Anonymous

The Painter's Manual

containing the best methods of, and the latest improvements in, house

painting, sign painting, graining, varnishing, polishing, staining, gilding,

glazing

Anonymous

The Painter's Manual
containing the best methods of, and the latest improvements in, house painting,
sign painting, graining, varnishing, polishing, staining, gilding, glazing

ISBN/EAN: 9783337293505

Printed in Europe, USA, Canada, Australia, Japan

Cover: Foto ©Thomas Meinert / pixelio.de

More available books at **www.hansebooks.com**

THE

PAINTER'S MANUAL:

CONTAINING THE BEST METHODS OF, AND THE
LATEST IMPROVEMENTS IN,

HOUSE PAINTING,	POLISHING,	SILVERING,
SIGN PAINTING,	STAINING,	GRECIAN OIL PAINTING,
GRAINING,	GILDING,	CHINESE PAINTING,
VARNISHING,	GLAZING,	ORIENTAL PAINTING, &C.

ALSO,

PRINCIPLES OF GLASS STAINING, HARMONY AND CONTRAST
OF COLORS, ANALYSIS OF COLORS.

TOGETHER WITH THE

PHILOSOPHY, THEORIES AND PRACTICES OF COLOR,
&C., &C., &C.

BY A PRACTICAL PAINTER.

––––––––

NEW YORK : —
JESSE HANEY & CO., PUBLISHERS,
OFFICE OF HANEY'S JOURNAL,
119 NASSAU ST.

PREFACE.

It is not proposed in the following pages to compile a work of " valuable recipes," which, if followed, would lead the learner into vague uncertainties instead of giving him any light on the subject. Works on decorative art are not generally written by practical men, and consequently are of no practical utility. But this *"Painter's Manual"* it is hoped will be found to contain the very best methods of practice in all that pertains to general painting, which methods are given in as plain and concise a manner as possible.

It is proposed, also, not only to give correct instructions in the art, but, which is of quite as much importance, instruct the painter how to preserve his health, by preventing the deleterious effects of the poisonous colors.

In describing work and preparation of colors, great brevity will be used; and the matter is as extensively classified as possible, the object being to make the work useful to learners.

Such a book is much needed in this country, for there is not in the country any work of the kind published which is of any practical use to the novice. It is hoped this will fulfill its mission.

CONTENTS.

6 CONTENTS.

THE PAINTER'S MANUAL.

THE EVILS OF PAINTING, AND THEIR REMEDY.

It has been said, and with much truth, too, that "House-painting might, with study, and acquirement of correct taste and more extensive information, resume its rank as a liberal art." There is no reason why it should not. It is an art, and should be recognized as such, and will be when the painter shall have sufficient interest to do something more for its elevation. It is at a low ebb at present; for, while the various other branches of the fine arts have their elaborate volumes of reference, and Art Journals of deep research and investigation, and latest discoveries and improvements, for the benefit of their artists, the house and sign painter and the grainer are left to their own resources, to catch what they may by individual experiment and the careful observation of their own mistakes.

Though America may boast of many excellent painters, who may not be excelled on the earth, yet they are almost lost amid the vast multitude of ordinary, indifferent, and miserable ones. The long apprenticeship and practice of the former seem almost thrown away, for they stand a very little better chance, in the aggregate of success, than others who have spent little or no time in the study of the business. A poor workman can and will work cheaper than a good one; and, consequently, competition comes into service, and the finished workmen are obliged to learn their trade more thoroughly, that is, learn the art of *slighting*, before they are able to cope with their competitors, and obtain, like them, an honest living. This spirit is caught up by the employer, and, in the rage to get everything cheap in this go-ahead age, the lowest bidder, without regard to quality, too often gets the job; so, many good and poor workmen naturally fall into that uncertain and unsubstantial manner of doing work that characterizes all the sham, slop-shop works of decorative art. It must not be understood, however, that these remarks have only a limited reference, for there are both painters and employers who well understand these practices, and whose correct taste — and liberal pockets — keep them mindful of the purity of the art of decoration. And, in justice to the inferior workmen, it may be remarked that it is not so much a fault with them as it is a want of facilities for learning. There are no published books of any utility; and then painters are very chary of their knowledge, and do not like to impart it too freely.

There should be a remedy for this evil, and there can be. Painters should be more communicative, and not be so tenacious of whatever superior method they may have acquired or discovered. It is quite a mistaken idea that one's business would be injured by discovering the secret of a superior method to his brother painter. If all this secret knowledge was more generally diffused among the craft, the benefit would be mutual. Knowledge should not be monopolized, but should be imparted to all alike, and all alike would be benefited. A better style of work would be the result of such a reciprocity, and better prices would be realized (which is a feature devoutly to be wished by a class of painters, who, as a whole, are no more than half paid for their labor, in a vocation so deleterious to health). It would require more time and labor, and just as many hands be employed, and the trade would then be worth learning.

However, one is not to blame, if he has made any discovery which has cost him time and money, should he wish to keep it a secret, or patent it, until he can make his money out of it; yet, in all minor matters, it is not only neighborly to instruct one another, but is really an honor to the craft.

The art of painting, in all its various branches, is, perhaps, under present regulations, quite as injurious to health as almost any other branch of mechanical business, especially house and general shop-painting.

It is supposed that painters, in the aggregate, pay an interest on their life of about twenty-four per cent. ; that is, they shorten their lives about two months every year for the privilege of following the noxious business, and getting a taste of the colic every other moon. In fact, it is statistically true that the average lives of painters do not come up to the average standard of longevity.

It is well known that painting is an unhealthy business; and to such an extent is this prejudice abroad, that it is with difficulty, in some places, that master workmen can procure an apprentice.

The house-painter is much more exposed, and liable to the poisonous effects of colors, than those who follow other branches, on account of the large quantities of vapor exhaled from lead and the arsenious greens, especially that most brilliant but deadly color, emerald green. This poisonous color, as all arsenious preparations will, gives out exceedingly large quantities of vapor, the inhalation of which will very suddenly show itself, and is quite often mistaken for some other disease, and frequently, by physicians, so treated. It causes inflammation of the throat and lungs, and produces, in different parts of the body, small watery pustules, which are exceedingly troublesome. We have known painters to be so afflicted with this affection upon their breast, groins, and armpits, that they were unable, for several days together, to move a limb without great inconvenience and pain.

In England, where much more of this green is used, it has been ascertained from actual observation, and the experience of physicians and other scientific men, that a series of diseases the most complicated have resulted from having the walls of houses washed, painted, or papered with arsenious greens. Cases have been known where whole families have been poisoned by living within the walls of such houses.

Copper, arsenic, and lead are exceedingly volatile, and those persons immured within the walls covered with them are so perfectly enveloped with the vapor arising therefrom that they are continually inhaling it, greatly to their detriment.

A very singular case (and a remarkable and unmistakable evidence of the noxious effects of arsenious vapor) occurred in England a few years ago. A family, a short time after moving into a certain house, were taken suddenly and violently sick. A physician was sent for, who pronounced it a case of poisoning from arsenic. The patients were relieved, but lingered on for some time, and, finding they did not recover their health, left the building. Another family moved into the tenement, and were attacked in like manner; still other persons occupied the rooms, and the same results followed, until, at last, it was alleged that the house was haunted, and Madam Rumor set about making up the legends. But science eventually got hold of the matter, when, by investigation, the premises were known to have formerly been occupied by painters, who were accordingly called upon, when it was ascertained that previous to leaving the house they had buried a large quantity of refuse arsenic three feet deep, in the bottom of the cellar. The deadly drug was removed, and people were no longer haunted with this arsenious ghost.

Almost every painter is familiar with the noxious effects of lead, especially when cooped up in a close room, with *drawn flatting*, and perhaps the keyholes stopped up. Few there are who can work three hours thus, who will not, on coming to the fresh air, almost immediately fall, or stagger as though they had imbibed something of a different nature from turpentine. This part of the business will soon produce the painter's colic, and eventually paralyze, unless much care be taken to guard against it.

In England, benefit has been experienced in cases of painter's or lead colic, both by those who manufacture and those who use white lead, in the use of sulphuric acid in very small quantities. One way of using it is to put one dram of acid into ten pints of table or spruce beer, or mild ale; to shake it up well, and allow it to stand a few hours. A tumbler-full twice or three times a day is used. Another way, not so convenient, is to make the beer as follows: Take of molasses, 14 pounds; bruised ginger, ½ pound; coriander seed, ½ ounce; capsicum and cloves, ¼ ounce each; water, 12½ gallons; yeast, 1 pint. Put the yeast in last, and let it ferment. When the fermentation has nearly ceased, add 1½ ounces of oil vitriol mixed with 12 ounces of water, and 1½ ounces bi-carbonate of soda dissolved in water. Fit to drink in three or four days.

The painter is often asked what the painter's colic feels like. He could not, probably, describe it better than to say to those who do not wish to try the experiment, that if the strands of a rope, while being twisted together, should be passed through the bowels horizontally, and the whole abdominal viscera be twisted with it, a faint idea might be formed of the lead colic.

CLEANLINESS.

The painter, in general, pays quite too little care and attention to personal cleanliness, and, thereby, to his health. One will frequently work for half a day with flatting, daub and spatter himself till he looks as though some one had been practising granite on him, and when noon comes, without washing, sit down in the same room where he has been working and eat a *cold dinner*, highly seasoned with carbonate of lead and turpentine! It is no wonder they are sick. Can any one imagine a reason why they should not be?

A journeyman house-painter of Boston, who was subject to attacks of the colic, applied to a celebrated physician of that city in the hopes of obtaining an antidote, or at least a preventive of this complaint. The doctor ordered him to pay particular attention to washing his face and hands, and rinsing his mouth before eating, change of clothing, &c. This course the painter adopted; but it lasted only while the memory of the colic pains was fresh in his mind. In the course of a year the order was forgotten, and he backslid from his cleanliness, until he slid his back upon the bed. The doctor was again called, prescribed again, which was followed by the same practice and the same results, and the painter was once more brought to bed, from which he rose not again.

A few years ago there was a painter in Cincinnati who was so used up from the effects of lead and abuse, that he was unable, sometimes for eighteen months, to walk; and during his best days he waddled along with such an uncertain, ungainly motion, that it was difficult to tell whether he was walking backwards or forwards; in fact, he seemed to be trying to do both at the same time.

Now the fault lay chiefly with himself. He was in the

habit of " spreeing" pretty often, and he confessed that he
had worked, with flatting, for three successive weeks with
no other nourishment than what few crackers he took to
" wash down the whiskey," slept in the paint-shop, and did
not wash his hands during the whole time. The greatest
wonder is that he could live in any shape.

The above is no guess-work, but the cases are *bona fide*
ones, and very remarkable, and we are happy to say *rare*
cases of neglect and uncleanness among painters; yet
we cannot help thinking that they suggest the idea that soap
and water are cheap and convenient, and are worth more
than all the pills and powders in Christendom.

Another great source of trouble is, suffering the color to
accumulate under the finger-nails, and there remain till it is
dry, and rattles out into the food, and thence into the stomach. Now an occasional dose of this might, perhaps, on the
homœopathic principle of infinitesimality, drive out of the
system the accumulated lead; but the mischief of it is, if
the principle is homœopathic, the doses are allopathic; and
as these two systems are at loggerheads at present, it is not
prudent that the painter should attempt in this manner to
harmonize them.

It is a very easy matter to preserve the clothes, and thereby
in a great measure the health. It should be a part of the
trade, which, when once learned, is just as easy to practise
as it is to swing the brush; and if the master painters
would have an eye to this, they would not only find it an
advantage to themselves, but a great blessing to their ap-
prentices. It is true that some are born with a natural
taste for the art — for neatness is an art — and some have
to acquire it; but it can be acquired, and should be, just as
much as any part of the trade.

These may be considered small matters to write about;
but let the *old* painter, if such a being can be found, look

back at the past, and he will tell you they are *great* matters.

Those painters who are confined to shops are fully as liable to paint-poison, though of a different nature, as they deal more largely in dry colors. And here, again, another error presents itself. Their shops are usually poorly ventilated, being oftentimes in cellars and basements, from which the vapors scarcely have a chance to escape, and thus the individual is continually inhaling the poisons arising from the everlasting messes of colors, and the newly-painted work; also by grinding and mixing.

Now the most of these troubles of the shop workmen can be avoided. In the first place, the shop should be well ventilated. It can easily be done by partitioning off a small room, or cupboard, for the keeping of all the colors, dry and mixed, from which, as well as the room occupied, a pipe or conductor should extend to the open air. The best ventilator is the *Air Siphon*, a late scientific discovery. It consists of an inverted siphon, which may be a tube of tin, wood, or other material, or a stove-pipe, six inches in diameter, made in the shape of a semicircle, or like the rounded elbow of a stove-pipe; the legs of it should be from twelve to twenty inches in length. This should be inserted in the chimney, with the two open ends up, the chimney answering for the longer leg of the siphon. All foul or vitiated air very rapidly escapes through this, thereby very thoroughly ventilating the apartment. This air siphon is highly useful for ventilation, and should everywhere be adopted.

In regard to inhaling the dust from grinding the dry colors, it is probably quite as cheap, if the time is considered, to use the colors which come ready ground in tubes.

It should be well understood that most mineral colors. when mixed with oil, turpentine, or any fatty matter, thro off exceedingly large quantities of vapor, which, being inhaled and passing into the lungs, is forced through the capillaries into every part of the system, giving rise to many unpleasant and dangerous disorders. A portion, too, is absorbed by the skin, but this cannot so well be avoided; the practical neglect and carelessness, however, can. The former Nature can combat with and recover from, but the additional force of the latter, with all its retinue of auxiliaries, is too much, and the victim to carelessness is, sooner or later, overcome, and forced to yield to superior power, and finally drops into his grave, or remains a cripple, and hobbles around in its immediate vicinity.

We shall now close this division by recommending

A FEW RULES TO BE OBSERVED.

Avoid spattering, for it is unpleasant as well as dangerous to be continually enveloped in robes of poisonous paint.

Never attempt to eat or sleep without first washing the hands and face and rinsing the mouth.

Wash the whole surface of the body at least once a week, with soft water.

Keep the buckets, brushes, &c., clean, so that they may be handled without smearing the hands.

Every painter should wear overalls, or change his clothing throughout once a week at least, in the mean time thoroughly airing those he has thrown off.

Keep the shops clean and well ventilated.

Never sleep in a paint-shop, nor in a newly-painted room, nor paint the walls of a room with any of the metallic greens.

Never suffer the paint to accumulate upon the clothing, nor under the finger nails.

Never wash the hands in turpentine, as it relaxes the

muscles and injures the joints.   Any animal oil, or even lin-seed oil, is better.

Never drink water that has stood any length of time in a paint-shop, or in a newly-painted room.

Never use spirituous liquors (except prescribed by a physician), especially when ailing from the effect of paint, as it unites with the mineral salts and tends to harden them, and causes inflammation of the parts where they concrete.

Milk, sweet oil, and the like, should be used freely, as they tend to soften the accumulated poisons, and carry them off.

Vinegar and acid fruits, used constantly, unite with the lead that may be in the stomach, chemically changing it to the acetate, or sugar of lead, which is by far the least dangerous.   Acetate of lead is scarcely recognized, in medical jurisprudence, as a poison.

Avoid breathing the dust when emptying papers of dry colors.

Make your smalts where there is a current of air ; and, while stirring, stand to the windward, that you may not inhale the smoke.

ANALYSIS OF COLORS.

THERE are several of the metals, the salts of which form a good material for painting; but that most extensively used in the arts is lead.

WHITE.

Nearly all whites have their base in the oxides and carbonates of different metals.

WHITE LEAD is a carbonate of lead, prepared by submitting common lead to the action of acetic acid, or vinegar, at a high temperature. It is poisonous, especially when combined with oils or fatty matter.

The chief adulterations are barytes, whiting, and silicate of potash.

CARBONATE OF BARYTES is less poisonous than lead; it is certainly not as valuable, and has very little body, though it is whiter, and when combined with lead in proper proportions, makes a very good white, and does not injure the lead for ordinary purposes. The sulphate of barytes is often used in the cheaper leads, but is an inferior article.

ZINC WHITE is an oxide of zinc. It is a durable and beautiful white, besides being harmless. All the very best and finest work in the cities is now finished with zinc. It has less body than lead, but is vastly whiter and more durable, and does not, like lead, turn yellow when excluded from the light and air.

CHINA WHITE is lead that has been elutriated, or washed, thereby freeing it from all impurities.

WHITING is well known to all. It is a carbonate of lime. It is of no utility as a paint, as it will become spotted, and rubs off after the oil is evaporated. It is properly fit for putty, and various room washes.

PEARL WHITE is generally used for the finer and more delicate branches of painting. It is a submuriate of bismuth.

KREMLITZ WHITE is a superior quality of lead. There is little in the market at present, as the extensive manufactories at Krems have been abandoned. All German leads are considered the best, as their ores contain less iron.

SILVER WHITE is also a lead prepared by elutriating. It is the best of the tube colors for general use.

There are various other whites, mostly manufactured in Germany.

VENICE WHITE is a mixture of equal parts of sulphate of barytes and lead.

HAMBURG WHITE is two parts of barytes and one of lead.

DUTCH WHITE, three parts of barytes and one of lead.

It will be perceived that these mixtures are of little utility to the painter.

YELLOWS.

Yellows have their bases in iron, lead, quicksilver, and arsenic.

CHROME YELLOW. The best is made from chromium and acetate, or the nitrate of lead, and is properly a chromate of lead. An inferior article is prepared with whiting. The best now in use for general painting has its base in silicate of potash and barytes.

GAMBOGE is the concrete juice of various trees in Ceylon. It is a transparent color, and consequently useful as a glazing color.

YELLOW OCHRE is an earth. The best comes from France.

STONE OCHRE is also an earth, found in many parts of Europe.

NAPLES YELLOW is an earth found near Naples, but most of that now in the market is composed of lead, alum, sal-ammonia, and antimony. It is a soft, bright, and durable color.

TURNER'S YELLOW, a muriate of lead. This is a beautiful tint, and has formerly been much used among coach-painters.

REDS.

Reds have their bases in iron mostly, and some have supposed that all reds are dependent upon the presence of iron for their color.

CARMINE is kaolin, or China clay, colored with cochineal, and, being prepared with much difficulty, it is very expensive. A common article is composed of alum and cream of tartar, colored with cochineal.

This color fades rapidly on exposure to the sun, and is of little use in out-door work. It is a rich, transparent color.

VERMILION is composed of sulphur and quicksilver. The first quality, at present, comes from France, it being difficult to get Chinese vermilion that is free from pulverized glass ; in fact, the greater portion of the Chinese vermilion now in the market is almost worthless in consequence of this adulteration. The English and American vermilions are cheaper, and inferior in *color* rather than quantity.

CHROME RED, or American vermilion, as it is sometimes called, though not so fine a color when first used, is much cheaper than vermilion, being one fifth the price; it stands exposure much better, retaining its hue long after the best Chinese has turned brown. For this reason it is much better adapted to all out-door painting. Its composition is saltpetre and chrome yellow, produced by a process of heating and washing.

ROSE PINK is nothing more than whiting, tinctured with Brazil wood, and is of little service in out-door painting, as it immediately fades on exposure to light. It is cheap, and being transparent, does very well for a glaze for chairs or other furniture.

RED LEAD, or red oxide of lead, is of more use in boiling in oil to make it dry than anything else. It is not much used among painters on account of its fading quality, though it is used in some compound mixtures. With chrome yellow, it makes a rich ground for mahogany. It is a durable color, and is therefore preferred by wheelwrights for painting wagons.

MADDER LAKE is the only lake that does not fade. A fine, transparent glaze for beautiful and delicate work, but too expensive for common work. Its composition is alum and soda, or silicate of potash, or kaolin colored with madder.

VENETIAN RED is an earth, found in various parts of the world. It is the principal body used for all common purposes.

BLUES.

Copper is the base of most blues, though some are formed from iron and cobalt.

PRUSSIAN BLUE is properly a ferrocyanuret of iron, produced by various processes. As a vehicle, dried or calcined blood and horns and hoofs are used.

There are other methods, where animal matter is not used, in which pearlash, coke, and iron-filings form the compound. It is also chemically prepared with sulphate of iron and prussiate of potash ; but in all these preparations the composition is iron and prussic acid. The prussic acid, however, is not in sufficient quantity to make the color in the least degree poisonous.

ULTRAMARINE. This beautiful blue was formerly made from lazulite, the beautiful variegated blue mineral, and was once worth, in Italy, twenty-five dollars an ounce. That used in the arts now is composed of carbonate of soda, sulphur, and kaolin, colored with cobalt.

This color has but little body as an oil color, but is of a most brilliant hue, and wears about as well as the Prussian blue. In oil it is a transparent color, but is more dense in distemper, and covers better.

GREENS.

All mineral greens have their bases in copper, and some of them contain arsenic.

BRUNSWICK or BREMEN GREEN is a compound of carbonate of copper and chalk, and the best has a portion of lead.

This is a fine, lasting green, and is much more neglected

than it should be. It is less poisonous than most greens, as it contains little or no arsenic. When used alone, it is of too blue a cast, but being lightened up with light chrome, or lemon chrome yellow, it makes a green almost equal to emerald, both in brilliancy and durability, and has a softer, pleasanter tone. An equal quantity of emerald mixed with it increases its brilliancy.

SCHEELE'S GREEN is composed of acetate of copper and arseniate of potash. It is very poisonous, without being redeemed by beauty or durability.

EMERALD GREEN. This intensely brilliant color is a compound of yellow arsenic and verdigris, and consequently the most deadly poison with which painters have to deal. Some years ago, when verdigris was in vogue, painters complained of the deleterious effect of that miserable color; but they may now well find fault when they are obliged to stand the ravages of the combined force of that and arsenic also. It was first discovered and manufactured in France, and has only been in use a few years, and it is to be hoped that its future existence will be as brief as its past; for its effects upon the people who have their rooms painted, washed, and papered with it are almost as bad as upon the painter who uses it.

CHROME GREEN was formerly made from the blue oxide of chromium, but that which is now mostly in use is a compound of potash, sulphur, and chromic acid. Some factories, however, are now preparing it from the chemical Prussian blue and chrome yellow.

This is a very soft, rich, and durable color, but in the rage for the glaring emerald, it has been much overlooked.

BROWNS.

Browns generally depend upon iron for their grades of tint.

UMBER is an earth found in Turkey and the Island of Cyprus. Both in its raw and burnt state it forms one of the best body browns we have. It is a valuable article in graining oak and black-walnut.

TERRA DE SIENNA, as its name indicates, is an earth found in the neighborhood of Sienna, Italy. Raw and burnt, it is a rich, transparent color. The raw makes a good grain color for maple and satin-wood, the burnt for mahogany, and both are good colors for glazing, and for shading on gold.

These are the browns mostly in use, though VANDYKE BROWN is useful in graining the darker woods; yet Terra de Sienna, umber, and ivory black are sufficient for all common purposes.

MINERAL BROWN is made by mixing equal parts, in water, of sulphate of copper and prussiate of potash, and then evaporating the water. It is a bright, yellowish, transparent brown, similar to raw Sienna.

SPANISH BROWN is a miserable, dull color, and not of much utility.

BLACKS.

LAMP BLACK is merely the smoke from various sub stances. The best is from coal tar. This is the best black for all common painting.

IVORY BLACK, or bone black, is only charred bone. It has not the body, nor does it work as freely as lamp black.

DROP BLACK. Either of the above may be washed, or

elutriated, and then dried in drops. It is the purest form, and useful in the finer portions of painting.

ASPHALTUM, although so very transparent, is, when several coats are laid on, a most intense black, but not of much service when exposed to the weather. It is best used dissolved in turpentine, slightly warm, with or without a little boiled oil. Without the oil, it dries very quick; with it, much slower. It makes the black varnish used for japanning tin and other metals. Gum asphaltum is gathered from the surface of the Dead Sea, or the Lake Asphaltites, in Judea.

Remarks. — The best colors are generally the cheapest. The best test is comparison. Look at the best and the poorest: the difference will be manifest.

SMALTS.

The glass smalts are made by grinding glass that contains some mineral coloring matter.

BLUE SMALT is ground glass, colored with cobalt in the furnace.

GREEN SMALT. There are no green smalts manufactured which are of much use. A bright green smalt may be made by heating white sand almost to a red heat, and then putting in, while hot, equal parts of emerald and Brunswick green, mixed with boiled oil and a little turpentine. A sufficient quantity of color must be used to color the sand a rich green. It should be stirred till nearly dry, and then spread out for drying, with occasional stirring till it is quite dry and well separated, and then sifted. Much care should be observed in doing this, as the arsenic and copper contained in the green will play the mischief with one's throat and lungs. It is best to be in a draught of air, and stand to the windward.

RED SMALT can only be obtained by the same process as above, using chrome red for coloring. The sand must not be heated so hot as for green. The sand for both of these smalts should be pure and white.

BROWN SMALT. A rather poor article comes in the shape of ground glass, but a better article may be made as above, using vandyke, or any of the browns, to color with,. changing the tone to suit the fancy, with chrome or venetian red.

BLACK SMALT. The common black sand answers well, and is much used for smalting. It is, however, a dark gray. If required to be a jet black, it may be made as above, using lampblack to color the sand.

FROSTING. Glass blown very thin, and then crumbled fine, gives a beautiful, sparkling, diamonded appearance to smalted grounds. The white frost is the best, and may be obtained at the glass factory, and sometimes at the drug stores.

FLOCK is the fine shearing of colored woolen cloths. It is greatly superior to any smalt, especially for in-door work,. and has latterly almost superseded all other finishes for sizing, &c. Almost any grade of color or tint may be obtained, yet the black is the most durable.

Remarks. — Much care should be used in making these smalts, by keeping them well stirred during the heating, and after they are spread out to dry, or they will be apt to dry in lumps. The best way is, after it is cold, to run it through a coarse sieve. Where any quantity of it is made, it should not be packed away for a few days.

Black smalt will keep almost any length of time, but the colored smalts will be more apt to fade and grow dull. These latter should be kept from the light and air as much as possible.

DRYERS.

JAPAN VARNISH, made with gum shellac, umber, red lead, litharge, sugar of lead, white vitriol, manganese, and patent dryers which have their base in the above, are all good dryers. Some drying quality, also, has been imputed to the onion when boiled in linseed oil. There may be some truth in it, though we have never found it of any value. The idea has probably grown out of the fact that some persons used to immerse an onion in the kettle of oil while boiling, as a test. The oil, when sufficiently boiled, would scorch the onion.

OILS.

Although many vegetable oils have been introduced to the consideration of the painter, yet LINSEED OIL still holds the preëminence for general painting.

HEMP-SEED OIL, CORN OIL, SUNFLOWER-SEED OIL, have all been well tested, and some of them work very well; yet they are not in much favor. They do not generally dry as fast, and are not so white, nor are they much if any cheaper than linseed oil.

TURPENTINE is the only oil vehicle that admits of the white lead retaining its purity of tint; hence it is adapted to painting white, where the work is excluded from the light and air.

BOILED OIL. The best method of boiling oil is to bring the oil to the boiling point, and then add from one half to a whole pound of litharge, or red lead, or umber, either one or all, recollecting that the more of these dryers that are added, the *darker* and more drying the oil will be.

Where a clear, transparent oil is required, add only sulphate of zinc. The tests for knowing when the oil is sufficiently boiled are, it will scorch a feather; it looks brown; it will crackle if a drop of water be thrown in; but the main thing is to cook it till the froth is all burned off. All these indications, however, will be seen about the same time.

OIL OF LAVENDER, as it dries very even, is useful where a hard, enamelled surface is required.

OIL OF POPPY is very slow to dry, but being colorless, is useful in mixing white and delicate tints. Sugar of lead or sulphate of zinc will dry it.

NUT OIL is clearer, but more costly than linseed oil; yet is prepared by artists for picture work.

MISCELLANEOUS.

LIME WATER. This great secret, called also *Harry Miraculous*, has been sold by travelling speculators for five, ten, and twenty dollars. Contrary to the humbugs usually peddled, this is a very valuable item.

Equal parts of lime water and linseed oil, which will mix if well shaken, when united with any body matter, particularly lead, form a solid and almost imperishable cement, which, for priming and second coating, or even the last coat, is far superior to oil paint; and the painter who supposed he was cheating his employer, was actually benefiting him. The color, however, works badly, as it is thick, light, and creamy, and harder to spread; and if fifty per cent. is saved in the oil, thirty per cent. is lost in time, and ten per cent. in the extra quantity used; so, after all, there is not much saved in its use.

PUMICE STONE, the lava of the volcanoes, is found floating

upon the surface of the sea.   It is a very useful article, which should be used much more than it is for rubbing down painted work.

FIRE-PROOF PAINT.   This paint is coming into use to a considerable extent.   It contains several of the alkaline, metallic, and combustible salts, and is, of course, to a great extent, fire proof, even when mixed with oil.   It works light, frothy, and soapy, and for this reason many painters do not like it.   It is cheap, however, and durable, but only fit for dark work.

VARNISHES.

Though varnishes are now made at the manufactories cheaper and better than home-made varnishes can be, yet for the sake of convenience a few methods will be given.

COPAL VARNISH.

Gum Copal, ...	8 pounds.
Linseed Oil, . . .	2 gallons.
Sugar of Lead, . . .	½ pound.
Turpentine, . . .	3½ gallons.

Boil till stringy.

Another:

Gum Copal, ...	8 pounds.
Oil, ...	2½ gallons.
Sulphate of Iron, . . ﹨	¼ pound.
Turpentine, . . .	5½ gallons.

This is a good varnish for house and sign painting.   In making the above varnishes, the gum should be melted in a small quantity of boiling oil, and poured gradually into the kettle containing the other oil, while boiling.   When it is all done, and cool enough so as not to ignite the turpentine, the turpentine should be added.

BLACK VARNISH, quick drying, and cheap for common purposes, such as iron fences and other rough work.

Black Pitch, ...	28 pounds.
Asphaltum, from Tar, .	28 pounds.

Boil eight or ten hours, then add 8 gallons boiled oil, and gradually 10 pounds red lead, and 10 pounds litharge. Boil for three hours longer, and add, when lukewarm, enough turpentine to thin for working freely.

This varnish will dry in a few minutes.

CRYSTAL VARNISH. One pint Canada Balsam, in a bottle. Set in a warm place till quite thin, leaving it uncorked. Take from the fire, and while thin, add the same quantity of turpentine. Shake till well mixed.

For charts, maps, prints, and all paper ornaments.

JAPAN VARNISH.

Gum Shellac, ...	2 pounds.
Oil, ...	1 gallon.
Red Lead, ...	1 pound.
Litharge, ...	1 pound.
Umber, ...	$\frac{1}{4}$ pound.

Melt the gum in a small quantity of oil, and then add it, gradually, to the other oil while it is boiling. Boil the whole till stringy.

This is a good, strong dryer, which gives to the paint a high gloss.

GUM ELASTIC VARNISH.

India Rubber, cut fine, . .	$\frac{1}{4}$ pound.
Linseed Oil, ...	$\frac{1}{2}$ pound.
Turpentine, ...	$\frac{1}{4}$ pound.

Add the gum to the oil while boiling. When dissolved,

add the turpentine. Boil the whole till clear, and strain.
Dries slow; if desired to dry quicker, use boiled oil. This
varnish is brilliant, durable, and makes the cloth pliable.

CAMPHOR VARNISH.

Gum Copal, ... 4 ounces.
Oil Lavender, . . . 12 ounces.
Gum Camphor, . . . ¼ ounce.

Heat the oil and camphor in a pan, stirring; then add
the copal in small quantities. When dissolved, stir and
add turpentine almost in a boiling state.

This is transparent, pliable, and durable. For varnishing
wire gauze, muslin, &c.

GOLD VARNISH.

Pulverized Gum Copal, . . 1 ounce.
Oil Lavender, . . . 2 ounces.
Turpentine, ... 6 ounces.

Put the oil in a pan on hot sand. When warm, add the
turpentine and copal, as in the camphor varnish.

TURPENTINE VARNISH.

Rosin, ... 5 pounds.
Turpentine, ... 1 gallon.

Boil till the rosin is dissolved.

WHITE, HARD VARNISH.

Gum Mastic, ... 1 pound.
Gum Anima, . . . 4 ounces.
Gum Sandarac, ... 5 ounces.
Alcohol, 95 per cent., . . 2 ounces.

Add all together, put in a warm place, and shake often.
When the gums are dissolved, strain through a lawn
sieve.

VARNISH FOR GLASS. Pulverized gum tragacanth, white of egg, equal quantity. Stand till dissolved. Spread on the glass carefully with a brush.

GLAZE VARNISH.

Powdered Sealing Wax, . .	$\frac{1}{2}$ ounce.
Alcohol, 95 per cent., . .	2 ounces.

Keep in a bottle in a warm place till the wax is dissolved. This varnish gives a beautiful glazed polish to paper, straw, leather, and the like.

SHELLAC POLISH.

Gum Shellac, ...	$\frac{1}{4}$ pound.
Alcohol, ...	1 pint.

Keep in a warm place till the gum is dissolved.

This makes a splendid polish for any fine article of furniture, guns, &c. It is best rubbed on with a cloth ; moisten the cloth with the polish, and rub over the work briskly. It dries in a moment, and twenty coats may be put on in as many minutes. It is also a good (perhaps the best) thing for killing gnats, and is altogether a very useful article, and no paint-shop should be without it. Rough and weather-beaten signs, cloth, and such like may be coated with it, which will make the work hold up the color better. Dry paints may also be ground in it, for painting signs on cloth or paper. It holds the colors from flying, and will stand the weather.

Remarks. — Any colored varnish may be made by adding any of the transparent colors. Oil varnishes, when too thick, should be thinned with oil ; distemper varnishes should be thinned with alcohol.

Much care should be observed in making these oil varnishes, that they do not take fire. If they should catch fire, have a board that will cover the top of the kettle ready, and place it on immediately.

GOLD SIZE. Various methods for preparing gold size have been adopted.

USUAL SIZE. Boiled oil, stirred up with a small quantity of litharge and red lead. Set it aside and slake often, till bleached; then draw off and bottle. Raw oil will do where a slow-drying size is wanted.

BEST SIZE. Raw oil, heated in a pan till it gives out a black smoke. Set fire to it, and let it burn a few minutes. Extinguish it by covering the pan over. Pour, while warm, into a bottle containing pulverized red lead and litharge. Keep in a warm place, slaking often, for two weeks, then decant and bottle.

BRONZING SIZE. Asphaltum, boiled oil, and turpentine, mixed in proportions to flow evenly.

INSIDE SIZE. Honey, diluted with water, vinegar, or any liquor. Glue size, beer or ale, white of egg, gum arabic, or any glutinous or albuminous substance may be used.

Remarks. — Oil gold size is thinned with turpentine. Lemon chrome yellow should be ground in the oil size.

Mixing Colors and Using them.

It is not proposed to go into an elaborate detail and minute description of divers ways and preparations of mixing colors and doing work, for the experience and taste of the worker only must be his guide; but it will be the endeavor to correct errors which have crept into use from careless and inexperienced workmen, and sundry " receipt books " which have been compiled by any but a practical painter.

PRIMING. Quite too little attention is paid to this department. The color is usually mixed up too thin and put on too heavy. The reverse is much the best. Let the priming be as thick as will spread easily, and then be well rubbed out under the brush. Litharge is the only drying necessary in priming. All work, inside or out, may be primed the same.

PUTTYING. After the priming, *all* work should have the nail-heads and cracks puttied up. It should be done with a putty-knife ; puttying up with the fingers is a barbarous practice, and does not fill the holes well.

SAND-PAPERING and dusting should be done before the puttying ; being done afterwards, is apt to dish out the puttied places.

SECOND COAT — *Outside.* Mix with raw oil, and use it as thick as it will spread easily. After the work is all covered, it should be cross-smoothed till it has an even surface, and then finished lengthwise, with long sweeps of the brush, pressing lightly.

THIRD COAT. Made a little thinner than for the second coat, and rubbed out as much as possible, cross-smoothed, and finished with the tip of the brush very lightly, so as not to show the brush marks.

SECOND COAT — *Inside.* Mixed as thick as it will work, with equal parts of raw oil and turpentine. Particular care should be taken to rub this out well, cross-smoothing and finishing with the tip of the brush ; else the color will lie in ridges, which the next coat will not hide.

THIRD COAT. Mixed with three parts turpentine and one of raw oil, rubbed out thoroughly and smoothed carefully, so as to show no brush marks.

FOURTH COAT — FLATTING. Mixed with all turpentine thin enough so that it may be spread before it sets. Spread over quickly, without cross-smoothing ; finish lengthwise

3

with light sweeps of the tip of the brush; three or four strokes will be as much as one can do before it sets. Square up and finish each piece of work before beginning another.

DRAWN FLATTING. Mix up the ground lead with turpentine, nearly as thin as for flatting. Let it stand till the lead settles and the oil and turpentine rise to the top. Pour it off and mix again, and repeat the operation till that which rises to the top is clear turpentine. By this process, the oil in which the lead is ground is entirely drawn out, and the lead is mixed with turpentine. This color, however, is quite different from what it would be if the lead had been ground in turpentine. It is more tenacious, and flows better.

Much care must be taken to spread this on thickly and evenly. The room must be kept close, and free from any draught of air, as the color sets as fast as put on. This is used only as a fourth coat.

POLISH WHITE. This chaste and durable finish requires the zinc white to do it properly. It is made by mixing the zinc white with white varnish.

COMMON METHOD. After priming and second-coating in the usual way with lead, finish with the polish white.

BEST METHOD. Put on two coats, as above, and then spread on several coats of yellow ochre, turpentine, and japan, with a little litharge. When dry, rub smooth and level with pumice stone. Then put on one coat of inside second coating, and flatten as usual; rub down with pumice stone, then a coat of polish white, and finish with a flowing coat of white varnish, in which is mixed some of the zinc white.

Remarks. — When work is to be finished with a gloss, the previous coat should be a dead surface; when it is to be flattened, the previous coat should have a degree of gloss.

Lead is the white referred to in the above descriptions, yet the rules given for mixing may be applied to all other colors, except that the darker colors are generally finished with a gloss, inside or out. They require no turpentine only when they are to be varnished.

Oil dries with a glossy, turpentine, with a flat surface.

It is a wrong idea to put on heavy coats of paint; the more it is rubbed out, the better will the work look and wear. Each coat should stand two or three days before receiving another coat.

Color needs more drying in winter than in summer. Outside work lasts longer if painted in cold weather, as not so much of the liquid is evaporated, and a heavier body is thus dried upon the surface.

Litharge or japan is a good dryer for outside work, and for priming in the inside, or for dark colors; but sulphate of zinc is only fit for the last coats on the inside, though sugar of lead is used. Either of them may be dissolved in water, and stirred into the color.

Transparent colors will work more freely, and spread on with an evener flow, by being mixed with raw oil and japan, with a little water stirred in.

In mixing thick colors, the liquid should be added gradually, else the lumps will not be thoroughly broken.

MIXING TINTS.

The first principle in mixing tints is to take the body color, or that ingredient which predominates, and add to it, gradually, the other colors. The principal ingredient may be thick, but the others must invariably be thin, or the lumps will spread out under the brush, leaving a streak of corresponding color.

In describing the manner of mixing tints, the predominant color will be mentioned first, the second next, and so on, as it would be impossible to give the exact proportion of each color used in any given tint. Thus, for instance, violet is mostly red, the next in quantity blue, and the least white, and so on. In this manner the following table exhibits almost every tint which the painter will be likely to require, leaving to his taste the peculiar tone : —

Table of Tints, and the Colors necessary to produce them.

Gray,	White Lead and Lampblack.
Buff,	White and Yellow Ochre ; Red.
Pearl,	White, Black, Blue.
Orange,	Yellow, Red.
Violet,	Red, Blue, White.
Purple,	Violet, with the addition of Red and White.
Gold,	White Stone Ochre ; Red.
Olive,	Yellow, Blue, Black, White.
Chestnut,	Red, Black, Yellow.
Flesh,	White, Yellow Ochre, Vermilion.
Limestone,	White, Yellow Ochre, Black, Red.
Sandstone,	White, Yellow Ochre, Black, Red.
Freestone,	Red, Black, Yellow Ochre, White.
Fawn,	White, Yellow, Red.
Chocolate,	Raw Umber, Red, Black.
Drab,	White, Raw, and Burnt Umbers ; or White, Yellow Ochre, Red, Black.
Bronze Green,	Chrome Green, Black, Yellow, or Black and Yellow, or Black and Green.
Pea Green,	White and Chrome Green.
Rose,	White, Madder Lake.
Copper,	Red, Yellow, Black.
Lemon,	White, Yellow.
Snuff,	Yellow, Vandyke Brown.
Claret,	Red, Umber, Black.
Dove,	White, Vermilion, Blue, Yellow.
Pink,	White, Vermilion, Lake.

Cream,	White, Yellow.
Salmon,	White, Yellow, Raw Umber, Red.
Straw,	White, Chrome Yellow.
Peach Blossom,	White, Red, Blue, Yellow.
Lilac,	White, with Violet.
Changeable,	Red, Green, lightened with White.

Remarks. — Any of the positive colors are made to any degree of lightness with white or yellow.

Colors for tints work best when mixed with raw oil.

All tints must be graduated by the taste of the artist, recollecting that practice and experience are great helps.

The finer the quality of the colors used, the purer and more beautiful will be the tints.

All colors should be ground before mixing, as the dry color does not stir in well.

CONTRAST AND HARMONY.

As the direct union of any two of the positive or primitive colors are harsh and unpleasant, neutralizing colors may be used, which, while they do not destroy the contrast, preserve the harmony.

One color will generally harmonize with another when both contain the same base in different proportions.

The choice and arrangement of colors in decoration should always be left to the artist, who should make these principles his study.

The following table, partly arranged from Alison, will give an idea of the principles of contrast and harmony, and will be found valuable in regard to the selection of colors for decoration : —

This Color	Contrasts with	Harmonizes with
White,	Black, Brown,	Any Color.
Yellow,	Purple, White,	Orange and Pale Colors.
Orange,	Blue,	Red-Pink.
Red,	Green,	Crimson.
Green,	Red,	Yellow.
Purple,	Yellow, White,	Crimson.
Black,	Pale Colors,	Deep Colors.
Gold,	Dark Colors,	Light Colors.

There is also an *harmonious* contrast, which must ever be observed in decoration, as it neutralizes the strong contrast of opposing colors.

Any of the colors of strong contrast may be made to harmonize pleasantly, by dividing them with a line of white, or any neutral tint. Thus, green and red, when placed together, may be made to harmonize if the glimmer be relieved by white lines which divide them. The width of the line should be in proportion to the size of the object, amount of surface, or the distance at which the object is to be viewed. There is great scope in the combination of colors, and the beauty of their arrangement, which practice, and a familiarity with their principles, will discover.

Some of these combinations of display may be seen in the annexed table.

WHITE, as a ground color, sets off well with blues, purples, violet, reds, greens, browns.

BLACK, with drabs, pink, lemon, gold, light blues, greens, purple, salmon.

BLUE, with gold, pink, salmon, buff, light blues, yellows, and drabs.

GREEN, with gold, purple, pink, lemon, dove, flesh, stone, pearl, light greens, and yellows.

RED, with lemon, pearl, gold, pale blues, and greens.

Remarks. — Light blues with dark greens, and *vice versa,* if divided with a line of white, pink, or pearl.

No two colors should be placed side by side, unless lined by a relieving color.

The placing together reds, blues, and greens, when of the same depths of tone, will always glimmer and look dirty ; but the harmony is restored by dividing their lines of connection with neutralizing tints.

When tints of barely a perceptible difference in shade are laid side by side, beginning with white, for instance, and making each stripe darker and darker, there will be no dividing line visible, but the whole surface, if a proper distance be allowed, will blend together like the tints and gradations of a sunset sky ; the tone is much purer and clearer when each tint is thus separate, than as though it were blended with a brush. Some of the beautiful frescos in mouldings, columns, &c., are done in this manner.

TRANSPARENT COLORS.

There are several colors that are natural transparents ; others that may be made so by mixture.

The transparent colors are *Terra de Sienna, Asphaltum, Dragon's Blood, Carmine, Rose Pink, Chemical Brown,* all the *Lakes, Gamboge,* and all the *Gums.*

Semi-transparent : *Umber, Vandyke Brown, Chrome Red, Emerald Green, Brunswick Green, Ultramarine, Indigo, Verdigris.*

Remarks. — These colors should be ground very fine, and spread on evenly.

If to be shown with a strong light, two coats may be given ; but if a subdued light, one coat is better.

Transparent colors are purer if elutriated ; that is,

ground fine in water ; let it settle ; pour off the top part of
the settlings ; mix that up with more water ; let it settle, and
take the top half of that, which will be free from all sand
and grit.   If the pure part of the pigment, however,
should be the heaviest, discard the top and use the bottom
of the sediment.   Usually, however, the purest coloring
part settles upon the top.

Any of these colors will work more evenly, and be more
transparent, if a small quantity of water be mixed while
grinding. ·

Turpentine makes transparent colors work crumbly.

Bleached boiled oil, or white varnish, is the best vehicle
for flowing evenly.   Raw oil does very well, only that
transparent colors are always difficult to dry.

Miscellaneous Items and Rules.

Under this head will be given a variety of items which
will embrace every department of painting, and will be
found of great use to every painter, — novice, amateur, and
master, — inasmuch as it is the experience of the best painters
in America.   Many of them will be found to be new, and all
of them valuable.   In fact, it is intended as a sort of *vade-
mecum*, to which the painter can at any time, when at a
loss, turn and be almost sure to find just what he wants.

KILLING KNOTS.   Glue size and red lead.   Gum shellac
dissolved in alcohol, and mixed with red lead.   Gutta percha
dissolved in ether.   But through all or any of these will the
pitch of the knot exude if exposed to the sun.   Perhaps
the very best method is, to size the knot with oil size, and
then lay a leaf of gold or silver on it.   In a very choice
piece of work, a hot iron may be held over the knot till a
good portion of the pitch has come out and been scraped

off, when the two coats of the leaf will be sure to keep out both the pitch and any discoloration.

KILLING GREASE. Old work is always more or less greasy and smoky. Wash over the smoky or greasy parts with nitre, or with very thin lime whitewash. Soda will do, but lime is the best and cheapest.

SOAP-SUDS, when used to wash old paint, should be well rinsed off, as it prevents the paint from drying, especially on greasy work. It will not sufficiently take the grease out; lime-water is best.

Any work that fails to dry, may be made to do so, by rubbing it all over with japan and turpentine — rubbing it well in with a brush.

PLASTERED WALLS. A coat of glue size before painting in oil. It is also best upon the white plaster or hard finish walls.

PUTTYING should be done after priming. Putty for stained work or naked wood may be made of glue water and whiting.

SANDING should be done on the fourth or fifth coat, and then a coat of paint on the sand. A pair of bellows, with the nose of a watering-pot upon the nose of the bellows, is the best way to sand cornices and perpendicular work. It may be blown on in this way without so much loss.

CANVAS AND MUSLIN. Dissolve a little India-rubber in boiling oil or turpentine, and add a little of this to thin paste while both are hot. This is the best size for cloth.

TRANSPARENT CLOTH. Stretch the cloth tight.

Pulverized White Rosin, . .	1 pound.
Bleached Linseed Oil, . .	12 ounces.
White Beeswax, . . .	3 ounces.
Venice Turpentine, . .	12 ounces.

Heat the first three articles till dissolved, then add the

turpentine while hot. A good varnish for curtains and all similar work. Varnish both sides.

WATER-PROOF CLOTH. Equal parts of yellow ochre and lampblack; mix with it an equal quantity, in bulk, strong, boiling soap-suds. Lay on as thick as the brush will spread. In three days finish with black paint.

ROUGH WORK. Any of the ochres or lead, mixed with coal tar and thinned with turpentine, make an excellent varnish for rough work, and is also a great preserver of wood from damp. Japan will hasten its drying.

BOILED PAINT SKINS. This is a very economical way of obtaining a cheap and durable color for all outside work. All the cleanings and scrapings of the buckets, and wipings out of the brushes, instead of being wasted on the wall, may be saved and boiled up in oil. The hardest and dryest paint skins, putty, &c., in this way are softened and rendered available.

A GOOD CEMENT for gutters and leaky places may be made of these boiled paint skins, if while hot and thick a portion of sand and fine lime be stirred in. It must be used while hot, and when dry will be as hard as iron, and as durable.

CLEANING OLD SMALT. Old smalt on signs, &c., may be loosened by spreading on potash dissolved in water, or wet wood ashes or sal soda; or, if not too old, it is best scraped off. If the potash or ashes stand on too long, so as to soak into the wood, the paint that may afterwards be put on will not dry well.

TAR may be killed, so as not to show through the paint, if it be well scraped and washed with a mixture of equal parts of turpentine and ammonia, and then a coat of gutta percha dissolved in turpentine.

HARD EARTH COLORS, such as umber, Sienna, and the like, are much easier ground, either in oil or distemper, if they are crushed up and allowed to stand in vinegar an hour or so. If to be ground in oil, the lumps should drip till the water is out.

SAPS will show if a piece of work of a plain surface be left half finished for too long a time. Begin no more of any plain surface than what can be finished before it sets.

FLATTING must not be touched up after it is once finished, or it will show a gloss.

GLOSS. Color put upon a gloss color will give the surface somewhat of a dead or flat appearance ; whereas, also, flatting on flatting gives a degree of gloss. It is best, then, previous to the flatting finish, to have the ground slightly glossy ; and for a gloss finish in paint or varnish, it is quite necessary to have the previous coat flat, either in color or in the rubbing down, though it must be understood that there must be a sufficient body of color underneath to hold up the gloss.

WASH BRUSHES in turpentine, and then in warm soap-suds.

HOT, STRONG LYE will clean old cans, cups, buckets, jugs, &c., from the dried colors.

SIGNS, and other small work, in cold weather, may be made to dry faster by heating at the fire, so as not to blister, and then placed in the cold to dry.

TURPENTINE has no specific drying quality. It hastens drying only by evaporation ; and if there be no drying quality in the color used, it will not dry any better than if mixed with raw oil. Lampblack, for instance, would not dry at all.

GOLD CHANGING. This effect in gold leaf that is exposed to the air, has been a source of wonder and perplexity. Beautiful gold signs have sometimes been spoiled in the space of a year, having the appearance as though every other leaf was copper. It is probably caused by the copper alloy in the leaf, and the smoke leaving a deposit of sulphur. When the size is too wet, and the leaf is rubbed too hard in spots, the oxygen of the atmosphere unites with the salts of the tint underneath ; perhaps, also, by some of the leaves being hammered thin in the middle. Where it is from a deposit of sulphur, it may be washed off with weak sulphuric acid, or even with vinegar.

GUTTA PERCHA is an excellent article, dissolved in hot oil and turpentine, for sizes, giving gloss, durability, and flexibility to varnishes. Gutta percha may be made available for many uses to the painter if experimented with.

PENCILS. Camel's hair and other pencils and fitches work better and last better if, when done using them, they are rinsed in turpentine and washed in soap-suds. When this is not done, keep them in raw oil.

RINSING CUP, made like a quart measure, having a small tin cup perforated at the bottom with fine holes, and fitting into the top of the large cup, and reaching down one third its depth. Fill the large cup with turpentine till it reaches over the perforated bottom of the small cup. Rinse the pencil in this, and the color settles to the bottom, leaving the turpentine always clear. Afterward wash, if desired, in soap-suds.

PENCILING BRICK. Straight-edged rules should be used as a guide to drawing the lines, perpendicular as well as horizontal. Drawing these lines by guess, as is the practice with some, does not fail to show itself in the want of uniformity. The lead for lining works best when mixed with turpentine ; used thick so as not to run.

BURNING LAMPBLACK is a great help to its drying. It also works better, and has more body. The best way to burn it is to pour upon it enough alcohol to saturate, then set fire to it, and let burn till it goes out itself. By this means the grease will be entirely burned out without injuring the black.

THREE COATS are required to bear up and cover. Two coats will not bring out an even gloss surface on any new wood, even though the wood be sized.

KALOSMINING. This process of coloring walls and ceilings is a great improvement on the old whitewashing plan with lime. You will first make a strong glue water, and while hot stir in whiting, and any coloring matter you please, till it is quite thick. This is the stock, and when cold is a stiff jelly, and may be kept for use as wanted.

To a given amount of water (hot is the best), add of this "stock" sufficient to make it the proper consistency for working. It spreads easily, and when properly done makes a fine finish for plastered walls.

ANOTHER RECIPE. A fine brilliant wash is obtained by mixing "Paris white" with glue, in the proportion of sixteen pounds to half a pound of glue. The glue should be the white, transparent kind. It should be covered with cold water at night, and in the morning carefully heated until dissolved. The Paris white should be stirred into hot water until it is of the proper milky consistency for applying to the walls, and the dissolved glue added and thoroughly mixed. This recipe is considered one of the best, and has the merit of being inexpensive.

OIL FLOORS with boiled oil, in which is ground a little litharge. The tone of color, if a color is required, may be made by adding any of the transparent colors.

MAN HELPS, made with a strip of plank or a broom-handle, with a hole in the end to admit the brush-handle, are very convenient to reach high and difficult places.

STUBBY-BRUSHES should never be used in turpentine color, as they spatter badly. They are only fit for painting hearths, rough bricks, or weather boarding.

CLARIFYING OIL. Various metallic salts are used. Sugar of lead, or white vitriol pulverized and well mixed with the oil, the whole to be set aside for two weeks, shaking occasionally at first. When settled and bleached, it may be decanted. Oil mixed up with water, then letting the water settle and pouring off the oil, is a very good way to remove any impurity in clarifying oil. It should be done in a corked bottle, as all clarified oils, when exposed to the air, become putty before they are done.

SHELLAC FOR PAINTING. Alcohol, with gum shellac dissolved in it, is an excellent vehicle to mix colors for painting ornaments or letters on cloth or paper. It works very free, holds the brilliancy of the color, and will stand the weather.

PAINTED CLOTHING. Equal parts of turpentine and spirits of ammonia will take out the paint spots from any kind of clothing, no matter how old, and dry, and hard, it may be. Saturate the spot with the liquid, perhaps two or three times, till the paint is soft, and then wash out all with soap-suds.

REMOVE OLD, HARD PUTTY. Take a brush or a bit of cloth tied to a stick, and spread over the putty with muriatic acid. The hardest putty in this way will soon become soft, and may be scraped off with the putty-knife. The acid should be well rinsed off.

VARNISHING.

All work, before being varnished, should be prepared with a dead surface, either by mixing with turpentine or by rubbing down with pumice stone. In very finely finished work, requiring a *level* surface, rub down with solid pumice stone and water; where only smoothness is necessary, rub with pulverized pumice stone with water, using for a rubber any woolen cloth, or felt, or buckskin.

THE FIRST COATS should be spread on evenly, and well rubbed out. Two, or four, or six coats may be given without rubbing; then, previous to the last coat, rub till the gloss is destroyed, after which give it a heavy flowing coat.

THE FLOWING COAT. Where work is to be finished on a cheaper plan, the rubbing need not be done. In this case give two or three coats, well rubbed out, and while the last coat is quite sticky, so as to make the brush drag through a little toughly, put on a heavy flowing coat of thick varnish — put on so heavily that it will flow evenly of itself. This, after thoroughly dry, may be polished.

POLISHING. Rub down with finely pulverized pumice stone till smooth and even; wash off. Then rub with rotten stone and sweet oil. Clean off the oil, and polish with chamois leather. Some use only the hand to finish with, which is quite as good after being rubbed with rotten stone and sweet oil. If the under coats of paint are not thoroughly dry, the varnish will be apt to crack.

GLAZING.

Sashes are primed before glazing.

Glass laid in with the crown or convex side out.

The tins driven in with a chisel or glazing hammer; four tins to each glass on the two long sides, about one fourth of the distance from the corners. If tins are put in the center, they are apt to break the glass, especially in cold weather.

BACK PUTTYING. In good work and medium-sized glass, after the glazing is done and the putty well set, fill the spaces on the inside. Use the putty soft, or it will press the glass out.

BEDDING, for superior work and large glass, is the best.

Glaze the rabbet with soft putty, and press the glass down into it as close as it will lay, pressing on the edges and not the middle of the glass, then glaze as usual.

Where the moulding of the sash is to go outside, the crown side of the glass should be out also.

CLEANING after the glazing is done, with water and a brush, or with whiting and a dry brush. The line of the putty should come just even with the line of the moulding on the other side of the glass.

RE-GLAZING. A sharp, square-pointed chisel is the best to take off the old putty. Potash is sometimes used to soften the putty when it is very hard.

The best diamonds are the cheapest. Those cuts which make the least noise are always deepest.

LETTERING.

If one has no taste for this branch of the art, it will be a difficult matter to teach him, by rules, to make a graceful letter or ornament; but, presuming that every one who engages in the business *has* a taste, a few rules will be laid down which will not fail to convey the right principle.

The following principles of lines from Hogarth are truly valuable : —

HEAVY LINES, when perpendicular, express strength. When angular or horizontal, harshness.

FINE LINES express smoothness and delicacy.

ANGULAR LINES are harsh and unpleasant. Therefore, the least beautiful lines are heavy and angular; the most beautiful, fine and waving.

All objects are more or less beautiful, as they contain this waving line, which is the line of grace and beauty.

According to this principle, the curved letters, such as

B, R, S, and O, are the most graceful, and the angular letters, A, V, and W, most harsh.

The most graceful form of letters is the Roman, or Roman fancy, while the most solid and substantial are the square block letters.

Though all the varieties of letters contain all these principles, yet the taste of the artist will lead him to make such combinations as will best please the eye, recollecting that all combinations, to be beautiful, should be uniform, not having strong, angular lines united to fine, waving ones. This applies also to all ornament.

UNIFORMITY.

In addition to these rules, uniformity must also be regarded, for uniformity not only applies to single lines, but to successions of lines, for irregular lines that are not in keeping are very unpleasant and unattractive to the eye ; and though the beauty of scrolling, or other ornament, is sometimes heightened by irregularity, yet the same rules of uniformity, grace, and keeping must be preserved, or the work will not make a graceful display.

From these principles we may deduce the following rules, as they apply to letters and ornament : —

Perpendicular and horizontal lines, with their angles, must be parallel.

Curves must hold the same proportional relation to each other.

Spaces between lines must be uniform, and in proportion to the size and length of the lines.

Perpendicular lines should be heavier than horizontals, and angles lighter than either.

The heaviest part of curves should be a little heavier in the center of the swell than perpendiculars, as a Roman O at the swell of the sides is heavier than the body of an I. They should also extend a little below, and very slightly above the line.

A true and well-proportioned Roman letter should have the main body four times as wide as the stems, or projecting points, and the length four times as long as the body is wide.

Block letters should have the horizontal and angular blocks a little narrower than the perpendicular ones.

The Egyptian or Gothic blocks are governed by the same rules as the square blocks, except that they are made without any projecting stems.

Fancy letters must be governed by the principles of the standard letters after which they are modeled; and the most perfect way to make a fancy letter, for the beginner, is to first make the standard letter, Roman, Block, or Gothic, and then rub out and add, still preserving the general outline or character, and thus alter to any ornamental shape that may please the eye.

GENERAL RULES.

In adopting a series of rules for lettering, it must be recollected that the eye, after all, is the most reliable guide; for, unless one has a tolerably true eye, it will be almost in vain to attempt to make a series of graceful characters. Two qualifications are positively requisite. He must have some artistic taste; he must have some mechanical skill. A knowledge of architectural drawing would be a benefit to the painter, yet it does not furnish the desired rules, and one may study geometry and mensuration for half a lifetime without being able to succeed in graceful lettering and scrolling.

The rules that can be given are but few and disjointed; no continuity of rules can be given that is not interfered with; for a rule, in its full application, that applies to one letter, will not to another; hence the eye must be the guide in the detail, as the rules apply only to the general character and outline; yet, irregular as these rules may be, if well studied, the learner will obtain principles which will not fail to aid him in this interesting pursuit.

The following diagram will give a very correct idea of the proportions of letters. Draw six perpendicular lines parallel to each other, and at equal distances. Then cut these lines with horizontal ones at right angles, making the spaces a little narrower. Then draw a letter upon the squares, by taking one row of squares for the stem, one for the body, two for the space, and so on, till the letter is finished, the dotted lines forming the letter, thus: —

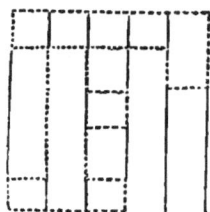
Block.

Gothic.

Roman.

This rule is best adapted to the Block and Gothic, to which it applies almost without an exception; yet it serves as a sort of general guide to the Roman. But it will be perceived that all letters do not require the same number of lines and spaces laterally. A block I, for instance, requires only three squares in width, while an M requires seven. Some again require half squares to give them their proper proportion.

The diagram on the preceding page serves to show the first principles of standard letters, but among the exceptions may be enumerated the following : —

The horizontal cross bars of A and G must occupy the distance from the center of the middle space to the center of the space below it.

The upper arm of the E extends downward a space and three fourths or a half, while the lower arm reaches upward two spaces, and outward, laterally, about one eighth of a space further than the upper arm. This is necessary, in order that the letter may be balanced, and not look top-heavy.

The oblique bodies of the M come to a point, or nearly so, at the bottom; it makes the letter more compact, and gives more room for the stems on the inside.

The lower upright stem of the S reaches up two squares; the upper one reaches down a square and three fourths or a half. The lower space, also, is a little the largest. The body of the S runs a little obliquely, being even with the lower stem in the left, and projecting a little beyond the upper stem at the right. The same rule applies to the Z.

The inside stems of the H, R, M, W, X, and Y are a little the shortest, otherwise the letters would be too much spread.

These rules and diagrams apply to all the standard letters ; that is, Roman, Block, and Gothic.

FANCY LETTERS

Are of every style, shape, and variety that the ingenuity of the artist may invent, yet to be graceful and beautiful they must be governed by the rules laid down for letters and scrolling.

It would be impossible to present a specimen of the numerous fancy letters that may be made from the standard letters. The taste of the artist will guide him in the curves, turns, and points necessary to form the standard letter into a fancy one. He will also find that one form will suggest another; and it is quite astonishing how many changes may be made by the combination of two simple characters, the curved and the straight line, — for all forms and shapes in art or nature are produced by these two lines alone in combination.

MEASURING AND RULING. Unless the eye be true and the hand steady, and both well practiced, measuring with the dividers, or other instrument, from point to point, the width of the bodies, spaces, &c., is actually necessary in order to preserve the uniformity of the whole work when finished. But the artist should not allow himself to *rule* his letters or ornaments, for it gives such a stiff and rigid appearance as will not fail to discover the unpracticed hand; in fact, no practice is sufficient to overcome or disguise the stiff and cramped look that characterizes a figure whose lines are drawn by rule and compass.

The letter, scroll, or ornament, when any degree of perfection is required, may first be outlined with chalk, and then corrected with the lead pencil or crayon; otherwise a rough outline, or a few dots, to serve as landmarks, will be sufficient: and the beginner should bear in mind that the less marking used in outlining, and the more careless and off-hand the letter or ornament is made, the more easy and graceful it will be.

The relative position of the letters on the board should be such that there is about the same amount of space between each two letters; thus, an A coming after an L, the two should be closer together at the nearest point than an I and an H.

The spaces above and below the letters occupy about one eighth of the width of the board, and the space between any two lines of letters may be a little narrower.

PUNCTUATION should be observed. It is quite as necessary to punctuate the reading upon a sign as in a book. There seems to be little regard paid to this at present, and the consequence is, that havoc is made of the "king's" English sometimes.

CREEPING of the color may be prevented by any means that will partially destroy the gloss of the ground-work, such as rubbing with the hand, breathing on it, rubbing it with a sponge or cloth with warm water, or weak soap-suds or turpentine, or, which is best of all, alcohol. Colors mixed with varnishes or boiled oil are most apt to creep when laid on a glass ground-work.

The ground-work of a sign should be, to use an old painter's expression, "put on thick and rubbed out thin." It is the correct principle in all ground-painting.

Signs, as all other painting, should be flatted for inside, and glossed for outside; though a little turpentine may be put in the last coat, for outside, in cold weather.

A good sign should receive four coats of ground-color.

The rest stick, or "mahl stick," in drawing lines; or the right hand may rest on the thumb of the left, while the little finger of the left hand touches its tip upon the board, and thus in turning, as on a pivot, the pencil has considerable scope.

Press the pencil down closely, and make clean sweeps as nearly as possible to the desired line, so that every stroke shall count.

GOLD LETTERS.

Care should be first taken to have a smooth ground to size on. Three or four coats will be sufficient; less will not do. The size should be limpid, and thin enough to flow freely and evenly, and well rubbed out, which it will bear if the ground-work be well filled.

POUNCING, to prevent the gold from sticking to the ground, may be done with whiting, starch, or rose-pink in a flannel cloth ; or the surface may be rubbed with a slice of potato, or with the white of egg and water, or anything containing starch, glue, or albumen in a small degree. However, whiting, rose-pink, or charcoal are the most convenient, and the most certain also. The pouncing should be very lightly dusted off after pouncing, and before sizing, with a blender, or other light, soft brush, or the size will spread.

SMALTED GROUND. Cut in around the letters with a color similar to the color of the smalt to be used. The color should be mixed with flowing boiled oil. The smalt should be sprinkled on freely, and if not very fine, like blue zaffer or the like, it may lie on for an hour or two, in order to give it a chance to absorb the oil. By this means the sign gets more of a body and depth of color. A very small quantity of white glass frosting, crushed fine, and thoroughly mixed with the smalt, gives it a beautiful sparkling appearance.

Flock is used the same as the smalt, except that it must be sifted on, and the flock must be well dried.

Shading, for the blocks or edges of the letter, may be

done with colors on the board before the smalting, but the most beautiful effect for the shadows and high light is produced by putting the color, made thin, on the smalt after it is dry. A fitch is the best for this purpose.

ORNAMENTING on the gold may be done with terra de sienna, umber, asphaltum, or any transparent color.

Where the letters come over any puttied spot, the puttying must have two coats, or the size will not stand out.

EMBOSSING on the surface of the gold with sienna, umber, &c., for the darks, and white, light yellows, greens, blues, gamboge, &c., for the lights.

ENAMELING, or gilding on glass. Outline on the glass with black or asphaltum, or other dark color, a fine line to enclose the gold; when dry, the glass where the gold is to be laid, wetted with water, with or without a *very little* white of egg, gum arabic, or alcohol, or whiskey; this last is probably the best, as there is sufficient albumen in it to hold the gold. The breath, however, is one of the best things where the gold is fine, and where two coats are laid on, for the first coat. In a few moments it will be dry; rub off, tolerably hard, with a piece of cotton or silk; wet again with a full pencil, drawing but once in a place, over all spots that are not well covered, then another layer of leaf; when dry, rub off with cotton. Fill the back of the letter with asphaltum, dissolved in turpentine. Two or three coats are necessary. When dry, rub off the surplus gold with a slightly dampened sponge or cloth; or breathe upon it, and rub off with cotton or the finger. After it is all clean, the shade or ornament, in color, may be put on.

When the ornament is to be done on the surface of the gold, do it on the glass before the gold is laid on.

ANOTHER METHOD is to lay the gold first, where the letters are to go, then frame through a pattern or theorem the letters with charcoal, finely pulverized. Trace with three coats of asphaltum, and rub off the surplus gold.

ANOTHER METHOD. Make a pattern of the letters of pasteboard or thin copper; lay this on several thicknesses of tin foil, and cut through the whole, making several duplicates; then coat these tin foil letters with a solution of gum arabic, and lay them on the glass. When dry, paint out the whole, glass and letters, with any color. Then wet and take off the letters of foil, and gild the places. A very pretty ornamental finish for these letters is, to put the ornament on the glass, where the foil letter has been taken off, with oil size, and then gild, when dry, with the enamel.

Painting with colors on glass requires two coats to make the surface even.

IMITATION OF STAINED GLASS. Paint the ornament with transparent colors. When dry, wash over the whole surface with sugar of lead ground in oil and turpentine, and while wet dab it all over with the end of a brush, very lightly; or lay a piece of muslin, wrung out in the solution, on the glass, and press it down closely; then taking one corner, lift it off. White lead may be used, mixed thin with boiled oil. Put on as little as possible, and pounce it all over with the end of a brush till it has an even ground surface.

Ornaments, cut of thin paper or tin foil, pasted on the glass, and the rest of the glass whitened, afterward taking off the paper or foil, makes a pretty effect.

It will be seen that letters must be done backward on the glass.

The white glass frosting, sprinkled over the ground-work of the glass while wet, gives a sparkling effect. It must be finely powdered.

TRANSPARENT SIGNS. Prepare the cloth with the camphor varnish (page 30); or, if large, like transparent cloth (page 41). Stretch tight, and prepare. Then key up the frame till the cloth is tight again. Cut the letters or ornament of waxed cloth, stick them on the cloth. Then with stiff, transparent color, mixed with boiled oil or varnish, dab over the ground-work with the end of a brush. It may be shaded with any dark color.

After the canvas is prepared transparent, any colored letter may be put on.

TRANSITION SIGNS. Cut into the band around the board grooves the width of a hand-saw, one inch apart, then insert strips of tin one inch wide, and long enough to reach across the board, thus covering the face of the board. When fitted, take them all out, laying them down flatwise, and with the edges close together, and paint any word. When dry, turn them all over, still keeping them in their same place, turning them over from right to left. Paint the surface of the board with any letters, pictures, or other figures. When dry, slide the strips, in the manner in which they lay, into the grooves on the sign. This sign has a very magical effect, changing from one sign to another as the beholder passes by.

REFLECTING SIGNS. Paint the letters on the naked glass backward, in gold. Then, when dry, paint on the back side of these letters any color. Then make a frame or box, the part of which will receive this glass plate. Then bed in the box two strips of looking-glass, the edges meeting at the center and up at the back of the box, the other edges curving up to the edges of the glass in the front of the glass, forming an angle of ten or twenty degrees, to the plane of the frame in front. Lay the lettered glass in front, when you may graduate the angle of the reflectors. It will show three signs at once.

JAPANNED TIN. Rub over the tin with cotton and alcohol. This will take off grease or other matter that may make the gold stick. Then sketch the design with white crayon; or, sketch the design on paper, and rub over the back of the paper with whiting — rub it over with a cloth;

lay the paper on the tin, and trace the design over with a pointed stick. Size and gild, and rub off the surplus gold with cotton.

SHADES AND SHADOWS. Shading is understood, among the craft, as representing two sides or edges of the letters, supposing them to be cut of wood or other material. It is done with two or more colors, showing the light and dark side of the object. The lines are all parallel with each other, except when shaded in perspective, when the lines of shade all run to a vanishing point. Place the pencil at all the corners of the letter, on the bottom and right hand side of the letter, and draw downward at an angle of forty-five degrees. This will give the outline of the shade. The perpendicular and horizontal lines of the shade are parallel to the lines of the letter. Make the shade as wide as is desired. All these oblique lines must make a corner with the horizontal and perpendicular lines of the letter. The high lights are put on the side, and dark on the bottom. These rules apply to shading.

SHADOWING, is representing shadow cast by the painted object, and is always of one color, and dark, and should be a mere glazing of the surface. Black, umber, vandyke brown, and asphaltum are good colors to represent shadows. The shadow will be on the opposite side of the shading. The different appearance of the tones of the shadows depend upon the color of the ground upon which they fall, for the shadow should be transparent.

Take a letter cut out of a block of wood, and paint it any color. Set it up in the window, and there will be readily seen the form, color, and outline of the shade, as also of the shadows. By this means the beginner may obtain more real knowledge in regard to the position and manner of shading than could be told him in a volume. By painting and gilding the letter in various ways, turning the letter edgewise, laying it down, tipping the top toward you or from you, will all give a correct idea of the form of letters, and the colors of their shades.

A trusty and judicious management of shading is necessary, lest some of the letters be thrown out of shape. S, B, K, and G, when they occur in a line of letters, will not admit of a heavy shade, else the whole inside spaces of the letters are filled with color. The shading should be modified to suit the letters in the line, so that each letter shall look free and easy.

Remarks. — POUNCING. A piece of flannel, or other loose cloth, filled with whiting, rose-pink, or charcoal.

MARKING ON GLASS. Wash the glass clean with alcohol and rotten stone, then give a coat of water and whiting; trace on this with a pointed stick, from left to right; turn the glass round, and paint backwards.

PERSPECTIVE LETTERS may be foreshadowed to suit the fancy, making a point of distance for each letter. The edge of a letter may thus be turned almost in front, showing the edge, top, and face side of the letter.

SHAPE OF PENCIL for drawing long lines or striping should be long and slim, and when used the pencil lays nearly its full length upon the board. For cutting scrolls and other ornament, the pencil is shorter, fuller, and when wet, has a sharp point swelling back to the center. For lettering, the same kind, with the point cut off square, but not too blunt. For filling up, short and thick. Camel's hair pencils are used mostly, though some prefer sable. They cost more, yet for heavy color are much the best, as they are stiffer, and hold the color without bending.

ODD FELLOWS' AND MASONS' APRONS, BANNERS, OR ANY SILK AND SATIN. Go over the whole surface to be painted with varnish, or egg and water. This will prevent the size or color from spreading. When dry, the figures may be

painted or sized in oil, and gilded. Where the work is not
exposed to the weather, or is required to be done quickly,
take white of egg with twice its quantity of water, or a solution of gum arabic; size with this, and lay the leaf while
wet. Where color is to go on, let the size dry. Colors
ground and mixed with varnish are not so apt to spread on
silk and satin.

Sizing should be tacky enough to hold the leaf, and dry
enough, when gilded, to rub down with cotton.

The following metal leafs are in general use: gold leaf,
silver leaf, French leaf, Dutch metal, and zinc foil. These
last two are of little utility to the sign painter. French
leaf, however, which is made of pinchbeck, when the work
is inside and at a distance from the eye, or where one leaf
will cover one letter, shows very well for a time; but the
laps of the edges, where two leaves join, soon begin to
show. It costs about one twentieth as much as gold.

Silver Leaf is alloyed more or less with some baser
metal, and consequently will not stand the weather, as the
oxygen of the atmosphere soon oxydizes the inferior metal,
and even the pure silver will soon tarnish when exposed to
the weather. It is about one half the cost of gold leaf.
These inferior leaves require the size to be more tacky than
for gold.

A very small amount of tallow touched to the cloth with
which the leaf is rubbed will take out the wrinkles, yet it
somewhat kills the gloss.

To clean old Paintings. A very excellent method of
cleaning and restoring old oil paintings, is to cover them
with wet cloths for three days, changing twice a day, and
washing them off at each change. When clean and dry,
rub them over with nut oil.

Tinseled Letters, or Chinese Painting on Glass, is
done by painting the ground-work with any color, leaving

the letter or figure naked. When dry, place over the letters on the back of the glass tin foil, or the various colored copper foils, after crumpling them in the hand, and then partially straightening them out.

ORIENTAL PAINTING is done in this manner. Various ornaments, birds, flowers, &c., are done very beautifully by using the colored foils. The copper foil can be had in the paint and drug stores all ready colored; but any color may be made with the tin foil (which is cheaper), by painting the tin foil with transparent colors, ground in gum water, or the picture may be produced by painting the figure on the glass with transparent colors, then placing the plain tin foil behind it. The background must be painted before putting on the foil, and then the foil may be put on in large enough pieces to cover the figure.

GRECIAN OIL PAINTING. Take any lithograph or other print, rub it well over with balsam of copaiva, thinned with turpentine till it is perfectly transparent; press it between folds of paper to get out the surplus balsam. Lay the face to a sheet of glass and set before a window, and paint with any transparent colors ground in oil, as near the natural color as possible. When dry, back up the print with white paper. The colors may be put on in careless patches, and when viewed from the front side has a very pretty effect. A few trials will be sufficient to show one how to manage the colors.

GRAINING.

This branch of decoration, like lettering, requires an artistic taste; nature, the eye, and practice being the best instructors.

In order to obtain any degree of perfection in the imitations of woods and marbles, it is necessary to procure panels or bits of veneer, and copy the color and form of the grains as near as possible.

GRAINING IN OIL. Mix the grain color in boiled oil and turpentine, and add a little soap, or whiting, or even both ; it makes it flow better. Clean the sponge, &c., in oil or turpentine.

FOR DISTEMPER, the grain color is ground in ale, beer, vinegar, or whiskey ; the object being to bind the color so that it will not rub off. As a general thing, stale ale or beer is the best. Whiskey, however, in cold weather, might be preferred, because it does not creep like other fluids ; but if the ground-work is rubbed over with whiskey it will be sufficient.

Graining should be done with a free and careless motion of the hand, yet having an eye to the character of the wood.

The descriptions of the manipulation will be as brief and distinct as possible, so as not to confuse the learner, and clog up his way with words.

DISTEMPER GRAINING requires the ground-work to be dampened by rubbing all over with a sponge wrung out of the ale, previous to putting on the grain color.

The ground-work : as in other mixtures, take the body color first, and add the positive colors by degrees, till the required tint is produced.

The work may be primed, as for other work, with any light color. The second coat must approach to the ground-color, and the third coat must be the tint to grain upon, and is best mixed with a gloss, either for inside or out. Less than three coats of ground color will not make a good job.

In particularizing the specific quantities of proportion of ingredients, we are governed only by general principles. The artist must regulate the tint according to taste.

The brush, cloth, or sponge, or whatever tools may be

used, must be frequently washed out in water while doing a job.

GLAZING colors are transparent, and are mixed very thin, whether the vehicle is oil or water.

BLENDING must be done by brushing the tit of the blender back and forth lightly over the work while it is wet.

BLAZING is done by sliding the blaze stick up, and bearing round to the right or left. The same motion is required in pecking in the fine check grain with the side of the blender; striking with the flat side of the blender, pushing the hand upward.

It is exceedingly difficult to describe the entire manipulation in graining. We therefore give a synopsis of the plan, and if the learner apply himself studiously, referring to this volume as a *Hand-Book*, he cannot fail to succeed, because the rules herein laid down he will find to be correct.

In copying the natural wood, it is the *character* of the wood, and not the particular individual lines and spots, that you wish to obtain.

MAHOGANY.

TOOLS. A sponge, or cloth, or a piece of buckskin for wiping out the lights.

A common paint brush, to put on the color.

A blaze stick, to make the bright blazes in the center of the branch. It is made of a piece of wood shaved down thin, or a paper card, three inches long and one inch wide, and very thin.

A blender, to soften the work.

A top grainer, to put in the dark grain.

GROUND. Chrome yellow and orange red lead. About one third lead, but sufficient to tint to a bright orange.

GRAIN COLOR. Burnt terra de sienna.

Dampen the work with the fluid you grain with.

Spread on the grain color with a brush ; blend crosswise.

Wipe out, with a sponge or cloth, the light parts.

Blend again till soft.

Put in the blazes up through the center with the blaze stick.

Blend down the crude roughness of this lengthwise.

When dry, rub off with the hand or a soft cloth, the rough particles.

Give a coat of thin varnish.

FOR GLAZING. Add a small quantity of asphaltum to the grain color, so that it is a shade darker than before, and add ale till it is quite thin.

Rub it well out over the whole surface.

Blend it crosswise.

Peck it all over with the side of the blender, pushing the hand upward to produce the fine check grain.

When dry, put on the dark top grain.

Another method is, instead of making the check grain, to wipe the blender through the glazing, making the top grain in that way.

Dark or light mahogany is made by using corresponding colors in the ground, grain, and glazing.

When the graining does not tint, it may all be rubbed off with the wet sponge, and grained over again.

MAPLE.

TOOLS. Brush, to put on color.

Buckskin, to wipe out lights.

Blender and top grainer.

GROUND. Cream color, made with white lead and yellow ochre.

GRAIN COLOR. Raw sienna and raw umber, equal parts in all. Coat the work.

Fold the buckskin, and with the edge wipe out the lights which make the curl.

Blend lengthwise of the curl.

Varnish with thin varnish, and when dry, glaze over the whole with the grain color made very thin, and to which is added a very little asphaltum.

Wipe out, with the sponge, large patches of lights, and blend crossings.

When dry, top grain with the glaze color.

Bird's-eye is managed the same way, except that, after the grain color is laid on, patches of light are wiped out with a wet sponge. Blend, and then dot over the whole, in patches, by sticking the ends of the fingers over it. Then blend very lightly.

BLACK WALNUT.

TOOLS. Same as for mahogany.

GROUND. Drab, made of lead, yellow ochre, venetian red, and black.

GRAIN COLOR. Burnt umber.

The grain is made almost the same as for mahogany, only that the blaze stick is used more freely; and by specimens of the real wood, it will be seen that the blazes run nearly the whole length of the branch, and more regular than mahogany, running gradually from bottom to top.

ROSE-WOOD.

TOOLS. A flat brush, sponge, blender, camel's hair pencil, and fitches.

GROUND. Drop black.

Spread on the color, and wipe out with the sponge or flat brush.

The grains are put in with the top grainer and pencils.

Glaze with rose-pink and asphaltum mixed, and wipe out any knots or shadows to suit the fancy.

OAK.

TOOLS. Brushes, cloth, and coarse and fine combs, made of steel or leather.

GROUND. Buff, made with white, chrome yellow, and venetian red.

GRAIN COLOR. Raw umber and raw sienna, lightened up with whiting mixed with boiled oil. There should be whiting enough to prevent the color from running together when combed.

ANOTHER METHOD is, raw umber and sienna, with boiled oil, in which is melted a little beeswax. Others prefer soap to wax.

Paint over the work, comb with the coarse comb first, lengthwise, then with the fine comb, with a waving motion.

Wipe out the grains, lights, &c., with a muslin cloth, holding it over the thumb nail, taking a clean spot of cloth for nearly every wipe.

Glaze with asphaltum, and wipe out large blazes of lights, and put in dark knots with a sash tool.

Remarks. — Asphaltum for glazing should be dissolved in turpentine, and then a little boiled oil added, to prevent its drying too quick.

MACHINE GRAINING.

Hand graining is now superseded in many places by machine work. *Adams's Improved Air Cylinder Graining Machine* being the one used for the purpose. This machine consists of an India-rubber cylinder, which can be filled with air at the pleasure of the operator, and kept extended.

Adams's Improved Air Cylinder Graining Machine.

The advantage of an air-filled cylinder is, that by pressure the minor inequalities in the surface to be grained will all be touched. The pattern is contained upon the face of a band or belt, of elastic material. This belt is slipped over the air cylinder and steel roller, the cylinder is inflated, and the implement is ready for use. The object of the steel roller is to make a sharp projection from the large cylinder, by means of which panels may be grained close to the ends. The pattern belts can be used with or without the steel roller.

With this machine, far more truthful and complicate imitations of wood can be given than the hand of the most skilful grainer is capable of, while of course the work is done with infinitely greater rapidity.

With this machine, an intimate acquaintance with graining is not necessary ; yet, here as elsewhere, the better the artist the better the work, for as the machine work is only used for the center of the panel, the surface at the side must be combed up to harmonize with both in the character of the wood and in the grain. The machines appear to be durable and well made, the graining bands being calculated, we believe, to last, with proper care, long enough to grain about one hundred thousand square feet. The machine itself will last a lifetime. A variety of bands can be had with the machine.

We have inserted this very brief notice here, as it is important to the trade to know of the existence of such a tool, but further particulars can be had by applying to the manufacturers, Messrs. Heath, Smith & Co., No. 400 West 15th Street, New York.

The following is a brief copy of Mr. Adams's directions accompanying the implement : —

The machines, when not in use, should be kept in a close covered box, and in a damp place.

Be careful to keep the rubber faces from coming in contact at any time with the handles, or any other hard substance.

The machines do not need washing, as the color that remains on them does not dry ; but they should be wiped off gently, after using, with a dry cloth.

Use the color stiff, but spread it thinly and evenly on the color board with a stiff brush, then roll the machine back and forth gently several times, and it is then ready for printing the work.

OAK GRAINING COLOR. Take equal parts of benzine and oil ; mix one pound of whiting, ground fine, to a quart, then add drop black and burnt sienna to the required shade. Glaze all over with some of the graining color, made thin, and wipe out lights and knots.

ROSEWOOD GRAINING COLOR. One pint of linseed oil and one pint of benzine, half pound of patent dryer, then add drop black, ground in oil, till it is as dark as you wish it. When dry, glaze all over thinly with asphaltum mixed in turpentine, to which add a little lake. Shade, and wipe out lights and knots to suit the fancy.

TO GRAIN ROSEWOOD IN STAIN. Steep camwood in alcohol, then mix it in thin shellac (dissolved in alcohol) till it is as red as you wish, then add a little dry burnt umber ; put on two coats. When dry, grain and finish as in other rosewood.

The price of the complete machine (two cylinders and sixteen pattern bands) is $100. They are for house painters' use. Larger machines, for coffin makers and furniture manufacturers, are furnished at corresponding rates. To manufacturers who make grained goods, this machine is invaluable. The work done by it is the best we have ever seen.

MARBLES.

Paint the ground-work, and when dry and rubbed down, dampen the whole surface with boiled oil, rubbed on with a cloth. For the light marbles, however, some prefer to work the grain in the ground color while wet.

Italian Marble.

TOOLS.   Camel's hair pencils, blender, and sponge.
GROUND.   Black.
GRAIN COLOR.   Gold tint, for bright veins. Burnt sienna, white and yellow ochre, fluid, oil, and turpentine.

Scramble out, in patches, with thin white lead, with a sponge; blend; then, with the hair pencil, trace in the larger dark veins with burnt sienna, then with yellow ochre, and lastly with the gold tint, running the lines over each other, yet all having the same general direction. It will be seen, from the specimens, that these veins are series of irregular loopholes and patches of light, crossed and connected by sharp, crinkled, and angular lines, the whiter lines being the sharpest.

When veined and dry, glaze with very thin asphaltum, in patches, to give it depth. Then varnish, and, if desired, polish.

Verd-Antique.

Tools. Same as for Italian, only fitches are used instead of pencils.

Ground. Black.

Grain Color. White, yellow ochre, and green.

Scramble in large flakes of white with the sponge, and blend.

Trace in the other tints in veins, something similar to Italian, only less veins, and more heavy, being done in large, irregular circles. Blend softly.

Sienna.

Tools. Same as above.

Ground. White and raw sienna.

Grain Color. Raw umber, raw sienna, white and black.

Cloud it over with a thin buff tint, in patches, using a sponge.

Vein with raw umber for dark, and raw sienna and black, mixed to a green tint, for the lights.

The form and character of this is similar to verd-antique, only the rings are more regularly round.

Blend lightly, and varnish when dry.

Gray and White Marbles.

This is very simple, though it requires some skill to do it nicely. Paint with white or lead color, and vein and mottle with black and slate color, in the wet paint, and blend it all down softly with a paint brush.

MISCELLANEOUS.

SHELL WORK. Ground with bright yellow or orange. Coat over with asphaltum, or any of the brown, transparent colors, though burnt umber is the most perfect for tortoise-shell. Wipe out lights with sponge or buckskin, or a roll of putty. Glaze with rose-pink or madder lake.

GLASS, grained in this manner, is very beautiful. Grain first on the glass; when dry, coat with the yellow; or, grain with gamboge and chrome yellow, mixed, and coat over with asphaltum or umber. Use the colors in oil.

ORNAMENTING PAPER is very prettily done by dropping some thin oil colors in water, a drop at a time. It floats and spreads upon the top in beautiful rings, and stands. Lay the paper carefully down on the floating paint, and it will receive the impression.

GRANITE. Ground with lead color, and spatter, first black and then white, over the work, by striking against a heavy stick which is held up close to the work. Use a stubby brush. The colors are mixed in turpentine.

STAINING.

Pine, poplar, &c., may be stained in imitation of the various kinds of finer woods, and, when well done, much resembles the natural woods. Previous to staining, give a coat of glue size. A very good and cheap method of

MAHOGANY STAIN is to boil one pound of logwood in four quarts of water, and add a double handful of walnut peelings. Boil again, take out the chips, and add one pint of vinegar. This does best for beech wood.

ANOTHER. Grind burnt sienna in ale or vinegar; make it thin; spread on with a brush, and while wet, it may be grained and shaded with the same, thickened up with more sienna.

BLACK WALNUT. Work the same as above, using burnt umber.

YELLOW STAIN. Grind and mix with ale or vinegar, aloes or gamboge; or, make a stain by boiling curcuma in water.

CHERRY STAIN. Good venetian red and glue water is quite as good a stain as the various decoctions, and less trouble and expense. A decoction of red sanders is sometimes used.

Remarks. — All tools may be obtained in the paint and drug stores by the names they are called throughout this work.

Glazing is a thin, transparent color, mixed up thin, and spread thinly over grained work or other ornament, for the purpose of giving the work more depth.

Where work is to be glazed, there is always more contrast in the lights and darks of the under work.

Principles of Glass Staining.

This beautiful branch of the art is quite too much neglected. The gorgeous display that may be made, and that
has been so successfully done by some artists, is sufficient to
excite the desire to bring it into more general use. One can
conceive of no more beautiful method of ornamenting the
windows of churches and public buildings, or, in fact, anything in the way of ornamenting on glass. The following
method is the one now in general use. Before engaging in
this, it would be better if the artist could get some little previous instruction. We will endeavor to give the correct
principles in regard to the oven, the baking, the colors, and
the manner of making and using them.

THE OVEN is made of fire brick, and arched over like a
common bake oven. This is to admit of an iron chest, or
muffle, as it is called, so close on the outside that neither
fire nor smoke can penetrate, and about three or four inches
less than the oven, so that there may be an equal space at
the top, bottom, and sides, with legs to keep it from the
bottom.

The sheet of glass to be worked upon (the softer the glass
the better) should be spread over with gum water, and let
dry, in order to prevent the colors from running together, it
being also much better than the slippery glass to work on.
After it is dry, lay it down evenly upon the design, which
has been previously sketched upon paper, and trace, with a
fine hair pencil, all the outlines and shades of the picture
or ornament with black. [See the mode of the preparation
of colors at the end of this article.]

THE LIGHTS AND SHADES are produced by dots, lines,
and hatches, very much after the manner of the engraver.
When this is finished and dry, it is ready for the

Floating. Take the prepared colors and float them on by dipping the pencil in the color, and taking it, as full as it will hold, to the glass, and just near enough so that the mixture will flow out upon the glass, care being taken that the pencil does not touch the glass, as it leaves a spot. This refers only to transparent colors.

Taking out the Lights. The methods of doing this, after the color is on, are various. Perhaps the best way is to take a goose-quill, made in the shape of a pen, without the slit. With this the artist may take out the lights by dots, lines, &c., to suit his taste. It is then ready for the kiln or oven.

Over the bottom of the oven, or muffle, must be spread, about a half inch thick, a bed of slacked lime, perfectly dry, and sifted through a sieve. Upon this lay a sheet of glass, then another layer of lime, and so on, if desired, for half a dozen sheets, though for very fine work, and where uniformity of coloring is required, it is better to have a less number. There may be quite a number of iron slides in the muffle, so that a number of glasses may be burned at one heat, without having more than one or two upon each slide. Close the muffle and raise the fire; but gradually, or the heat will break the glass.

After it is got up to a red heat, it may remain so for two, three, or four hours, according to the tests, which are strips of glass, painted with the same colors as the sheets, and drawn out occasionally. When the colors are properly burned in, the fire may die away gradually, as it was raised. When cold, the glass is taken out and well cleaned.

The chemicals mentioned in the following preparation of colors, may be had at most of the first-class drug stores. These preparations should be combined, so that each shall require about the same amount of heating to bring out the color.

Colors for Staining Glass.

FLESH.

Red Lead, ... 1 ounce.
Red Enamel, . . . 2 ounces.

Grind to a fine powder; work it up with alcohol, on a flag stone. Requires slight baking.

BLACK.

Iron scales, ... 14½ ounces.
White Crystal Glass, . . 2 ounces.
Antimony, ... 1 ounce.
Manganese, ... ½ ounce.

Pound fine, and grind in strong vinegar.

BRILLIANT BLACK.

Made to any degree of depth by the mixture of cobalt with the oxides of iron and manganese.

BROWN.

White Glass, ... 1 ounce.
Manganese, ... ½ ounce.

RICH BROWN.

Oxide of Platinum.

RED.

Red Chalk, ... 1 ounce.
White, hard Enamel, . . 2 ounces.
Peroxide of Copper, . . . 1 drachm.

FINE RED.

Rust of Iron, . . . 2 ounces.
Glass of Antimony, . . . 2 ounces.
Litharge, ... 2 ounces.
Sulphuret of Silver, . . . ½ drachm.

GREEN.

Brass Dust, ...	2 ounces.
Red Lead, ...	2 ounces.
White Sand, ...	8 ounces.

Calcine the brass to an oxide, and make all into a fine powder. Heat in a crucible one hour, in a hot oven. When cold, grind in a brass mortar.

GREEN. Oxide of Chrome.

GREEN. Blue on one side, yellow on the other.

YELLOW. Fine silver, dissolved in nitric acid. Dilute with plenty of water. Pour in a strong solution of salt, and the silver, in the form of chloride of silver, will fall to the bottom in a yellow powder. When settled, pour off the fluid; fill up with water; when settled, pour off again, and so on for five or six times. When dry, mix the powder with three times its weight in pipe clay, well burned and pounded. Paint on the back of the glass.

YELLOW. Sulphuret of silver, glass of antimony, and burnt yellow ocher.

YELLOW. Chloride of silver, oxide of zinc, white clay, and rust of iron.

It is by far the best method to buy the colors, if possible, ready prepared. Some, however, . *must* be manufactured by the artist. Among them are, —

BLUE. Oxide of cobalt, which is cobalt ore, after being well roasted, is dissolved in diluted nitric acid. Add considerable water, and pour into it a strong solution of carbonate of soda. A carbonate of cobalt is thrown to the bottom in a powder. Wash well, as for chloride of silver, and let dry. Mix this with three times its weight of saltpeter. Burn this mixture in a crucible, by putting a red hot coal to it. Heat, wash, and dry it. Three pints of this to one of a flux made of white sand, borax, saltpeter, and a very little chalk, melted together for an hour, and then ground into an enamel powder for use. Any shade may be had by more or less flux.

VIOLET.

Black Oxide of Manganese, .	1 ounce.
Zaffer, ...	1 ounce.
Pounded White Glass, . .	10 ounces.
Red Lead, ...	1 ounce.

Mix, fuse, and grind.

Remarks. — The fluxes are made of flint glass, borax, pipe clay, white sand, &c.

The principles of glass staining, and making the colors, therefore, will be found of great service to beginners; yet it must be understood that the practice will be very difficult, without some practical instructions; yet, one who has a taste, and some scientific ability, may be enabled, by studying these rules closely, and by a few trials in experimenting, to succeed in producing the work properly.

Rules for Measuring Painter's Work.

In regard to measuring work, it is generally understood that the measurer's judgment must be exercised to a great xtent. Hence, all work that may not come under any of hese heads, must be left entirely to him.

The following rules are given as sort of landmarks, and are intended to aid the painter not only in the measurement after the work is finished, but in making out bills and propositions for work, and they will also enable him to guess at the value of a job. The price, however, or the amount of deduction on this full bill, may be made according to the prices of material and wages; for at some seasons both wages and material, as also living, are much cheaper than others, consequently a per cent. on or off the bill may s)mo times be necessary.

PRICES PER SQUARE YARD.

Common Cheap Colors, —

First coat, ...	10 cents.
Second coat, ...	5 cents.
Third coat, ...	4 cents.
Fourth coat, ...	4 cents.

Blues, Chrome Yellow, Light Green, —

First coat, ...	14 cents.
Second coat, ...	10 cents.
Third coat, ...	7 cents.
Fourth coat, ...	7 cents.

Dark Green, Emerald, and other Costly Colors, —

First coat, ...	16 cents.
Second coat, ...	14 cents.
Third coat, ...	9 cents.
Fourth coat, ...	8 cents.

Sanding, ...	8 cents.
One coat over the sand, . .	14 cents.
Second coat over the sand, . .	9 cents.
Oiling brick, ...	6 cents.
Penciling brick, ...	12 cents.

Painting on Brick, —

First coat, ...	18 cents.
Second coat, ...	10 cents.
Third coat, ...	8 cents.
Fourth coat, ...	8 cents.

Other costly colors, per yard, extra, from 8 to 15 cents, according to the cost of the color and roughness of the work.

Graining, per square yard, for fair jobs, $1.00; varying, however, according to the amount and quality of labor, adding or deducting 50 cents.

Polishing, per square yard, 60 cents.

Puttying, for all work, add 5 per cent.

Sand-papering and cleaning, 5 per cent.

GIRTHING OR MEASURING.

Plain cornices, boxing, &c., girth once and a half, or one half its measurement added.

Block and dentile, or other equivalent ornament, once, twice, or three times its measurement added, according to the difficulty of the labor.

All other ornament, difficult to paint or to get at, measure from once to five times its real girth.

Barge boards, water spouts, gutters, &c., measure three times.

Paling and railed gates, measure and a half, that is, three heights, besides girthing the rails and posts of the railing, if done with one color; but if the pales are topped with another color, one foot extra.

All stone facias, window and door arches, and sills, double.

Window and door frames, in and outside, double.

Venetian shutters, double the measure of plain work.

Post and railed fences to be girthed both post and rails, and one half more added to the girth.

Window bars shall be measured square. Window sash the same, if done with one color; but if done with two, they shall be double measure.

Corner strips on frame houses, if painted with a different color from the weather-boards, to girth double.

Rough weather-boarding and old roofs, double measure.

Oiling and penciling on brick work shall be measured

square, and on dead walls, from one fifth to one third added to the measurement.

Balusters (either inside or outside), to be measured three sides ; if the hand rail is capped with a different color, one foot more to be added.

Corner strips, corner beads, and single architraves, double ; double architraves, girth three times.

Pilasters, two or three times.

String boards to girth twice.

Wash boards, base boards, &c., double ; capped with another color, six inches added.

Mouldings, measure twice and three times, according to work.

Base, or stair-case, twice and a half.

Panels, to be allowed two inches in height and breadth for each panel ; but if the panels are done with one color and stiles of another, measure and half ; if the mouldings are done with another color, double measure.

Edges of plain shelves, three inches girth ; beaded or otherwise, from three to six inches girth.

Painting on plastering shall be measured square, and the openings deducted ; making suitable allowance for cutting edges, and one third added to the measurement.

Sizing the walls of plastering, three cents per square yard.

All beads or grooves, too narrow to measure, one inch added for each.

All picked out work, to be valued according to trouble.

All work not herein expressed, to be measured according to the judgment of the measurer.

6

RULES FOR MEASURING BRICK WORK.

All painting on brick shall be measured square, and the openings deducted, that is to say, the actual opening which the sash or door occupies, allowing the thickness of the door or window-frames to make up for the reveals; if the frames or reveals are of an uncommon thickness or depth, a proper allowance shall be made by the measurer. If the stone or brick caps or arches are or are not painted the same color as the wall, there shall be no change from the above rule; but if they are painted with a different color, they shall be called from one to two feet girth, the price to be according to color, and number of coats of that color. If the stone sills are done with a different or with the same color as the wall, they shall be called from one to two feet girth, according to color and number of coats. Stone or brick facias and water-tables, if done with the same color as the wall, they shall be measured in with it; but if painted with a different color, they shall be measured the same as stone sills, &c.

N. B. No reference is to be had to the above rules for measuring stone facias, &c., where the walls are not painted.

PRICES FOR GLAZING.

Prices for glazing new sash, and furnishing the putty:

8 by 10, per light,	4 cents.
9 or 10 by 12, per light,	6¼ cents.
10 by 14 or 15, per light,	8 cents.
11 by 15, per light,	9 cents.
11 by 16, per light,	10 cents.
12 by 16 or 18, per light,	12½ cents.
14 by 20, per light,	16 cents.
16 by 22, per light,	20 cents.

When the glazier furnishes the glass, the usual retail prices shall be charged. If there is a percentage taken off the bill, the charge for the glass shall not be subject to it.

When the glass is bedded, the glazing shall be doubled. If back-puttied, price and a half.

Prices for glazing old sash, and furnishing the glass and putty :

8 by 10, per light, . . .	12½ cents.
9 or 10 by 12, per light, . .	18¾ cents.
10 by 14 or 16, per light, .	25 cents.
11 by 15, per light, . .	31¼ cents.
11 by 16, per light, . . .	37½ cents.
12 by 16 or 18, per light, .	50 cents.
14 by 20, per light, .	$1.00.
16 by 22, per light, . .	$1.25.

When the glass is furnished, the usual retail prices shall be deducted from the above. If there is a percentage taken off the bill, the charge for the glass shall not be subject to it.

PRICES OF SIGN PAINTING.

Lettering is measured running measure, measuring the length of each line of letters, without regard to their heights.

Plain letters, per foot, . .	30 cents.
One shade, add . . .	10 cents.
Double shade, add . . .	20 cents.
Gold letters, per foot, . .	$1.00.

Shading, the same as other letters.

Other fancy and ornamental letters and shading, shading on the surface of the gold, add according to labor, being guided by the standard.

Japanned tin, in gold, running measure, per inch, 7 cents.

Shading, per inch, 2 cents.

Lettering on glass, running measure, per inch, 7 cents.

Colored letters on glass, tin, stone, or other columns, and all small boards, running measure, per inch, 3 cents.

Dashes and other plain ornaments, measured as letters.

Gold borders, per square inch, 3 cents.

In gilding plain surfaces, the labor is equal to the cost of the gold. Ornaments in proportion to the labor.

These rules will serve as a guide in proportioning the prices to the amount of labor. It would take a volume to adapt a full list of prices to meet every variety of lettering and ornamenting; and these prices may be considered as a standard, subject to being modified to suit the amount of cost and labor.

INDEX.

(85)

BAD MEMORY MADE GOOD AND A Good Memory Made Better. This little volume will show how to systematize and train the Memory in such a manner that figures, dates, facts, names, and in short almost *everything* that it is desired to recollect may be remembered with ease. The method is not very difficult to learn, and by its aid the most wonderful power of memory is acquired. The power is astonishing to those who do not know its secret. The following items, among its contents, will give an idea of the scope of this work : How to remember any number of words after one reading; how to remember a series of words from different pages of a book, so as to be able to tell the page; how to remember figures generally; how to repeat a hundred figures, selected at random, after hearing them once; how to remember dates; how to remember poetry, prose, reporting, extempore speaking, chapters and verses from the Bible; remembering a variety of errands, messages, etc., latitudes and longitudes, etc. Memory applied to chemistry, grammar, geography, botany, with other studies. Training the memory; "stage memory;" impaired memory; and many things of interest on the subject. The foregoing gives but a slight outline of the contents of the work, which will be found a valuable one for all who desire to improve their memories. Teachers will find it of great assistance in their profession, and students, especially when preparing for examination, will find it a valuable aid. The information in regard to "speaking without notes" will often save clergymen, lecturers, and speakers, much tedious preparation and materially assist them in their delivery. This work is written in simple style so as to be easily understood and everything is made perfectly plain. Even children can be taught the method. After instructing his readers "how to *remember*," the author tells them "how to *forget*," and though this last accomplishment is given more as a curiosity in memory it may some time be of use. *15* cts.

HANDBOOK OF DOMINOES.—THOSE who have hitherto looked upon Dominoes as a very tame source of amusement will be surprised on reading this little book, to find how many different games may be played and how much real enjoyment is to be derived from Dominoes, which, when properly understood, admit of nearly as much variety as do cards. The Handbook is the only work which gives descriptions and full directions for playing *all* games of Dominoes, including all those recently invented, and the very popular European ones. *15* cts.

JESSE HANEY & CO., Publishers,
119 Nassau street, New York.

HANEY'S GUIDE TO AUTHORSHIP, A

valuable aid to all who desire to engage in literary pursuits of any kind, for pleasure or profit. Containing concise and practical instruction in the various kinds of prose and poetic composition; sensible advice on all points where difficulty is usually encountered by inexperienced writers; hints for overcoming natural defects and achieving success; in short sound and useful information on the various subjects pertaining to the art of authorship. The book also contains chapters on proof reading, punctuation, editing, estimates of the cost of printing and publishing, preparation, value, and disposal of MS., copyrights and legal rights of authors and publishers, and other matter useful to professional and amateur writers. **50 cents.**

PHONOGRAPHIC HANDBOOK, FOR

self instruction in the modern, perfected and simplified art of shorthand writing as practised by practical reporters. This is the only cheap book teaching shorthand as at present used, with the recent improvements. The old difficulties and contradictions are done away with, and the learner has only a fractional part of the labor involved in learning the old, and now seldom used, methods. Phonography is useful to every person, and no one having any spare time should fail to learn it. **25 cents.**

COMMON SENSE COOK BOOK, a reliable

guide for the preparation of a wide range of dishes suiting all tastes and all purses. One decided attraction is the number of delicious but inexpensive preparations which are included in the work. It is free from those errors so common and so aggravating in many even high priced books, and the proportions of ingredients are carefully given, as well as their manipulation and proper serving up. The book contains a very large amount of matter for the price, and even if you already possess a good cook book, you cannot fail to find many things in this one amply worth the price. **30 cts.**

HANDBOOK OF VENTRILOQUISM, and

how to make the Magic Whistle. **15 cts.**
"Really a valuable aid."—*Boston Wide World.*—"Will enable any one to produce the most wonderful vocal illusions."—*N. Y. Atlas.*

JESSE HANEY & CO., 119 Nassau-st., N. Y.

ART OF TRAINING ANIMALS.

A COMPLETE INSTRUCTOR

For breaking, training, and educating all kinds of Wild and Domestic Animals, tells how to subdue refractory and vicious animals, and how to teach animals to perform various amusing tricks. It also contains full instructions for training Song and Talking Birds, as well as explaining the mysteries of the Performing Canaries, and other birds.

It tells all about horse breaking, horse training, performing horses and ponies, mules, both serious and " comic," hunting dogs, performing dogs, shepherd dogs, trained cats ; how wild animals are tamed and taught to perform, with much curious information, dens of wild beasts and " lion kings ;" performing leopards, tigers, lions, &c.; elephants, bears, monkeys, goats, buffaloes, "happy families," snake charming and performing snakes ; tame and performing rats and mice ; singing, talking and performing birds, performing insects, fleas and flies ; and much additional matter that is either curious, amusing, or instructive Every one who has witnessed the wonderful performances at shows and public exhibitions, will have his curiosity as to how the animals are taught, fully gratified. Every farmer and animal owner, as well as every boy who wishes to amuse himself and astonish his friends by training some favorite pony, dog or other pet, should get this book. The instructions for teaching birds will prove very useful to every lady who keeps these delightful companions, and would alone be worth the price of the entire book. Aside from the value of the information contained in the volume for practical purposes, the book is one of the most readable and entertaining that has ever appeared. It is *not* a collection of stale anecdotes copied from primers and juvenile periodicals, but everything is fresh and new. Many writers have told of the wonderful exploits which various animals have accomplished, but no one before has told how these animals were taught, or how you can teach your animals to do the same. The book is illustrated with a large number of engravings.

In Press, ready September, 1866

www.ingramcontent.com/pod-product-compliance
Lightning Source LLC
Chambersburg PA
CBHW031443270326
41930CB00007B/842